The God I Left Behind

A journey from fundamentalism to faith

The God I Left Behind

A journey from fundamentalism to faith

By Brian C. Holley

श्रद्धा

Shraddha Books
Weobley, Herefordshire, U.K.

Other Publications by the Author

Why Silence?

Practically everyone who experiences 'soul-silence' speaks of it as the place in which they encounter their true selves. This little book offers a guide to finding this experience, whether you are a Quaker or not.

Available from The Quaker Bookshop
https://bookshop.quaker.org.uk/

From the Secret Cave

☆☆☆☆☆

'An expression of wisdom, ancient and modern, to bring meaning to those of us who live among the chaos of the 21st century.'

170 Sutras derived from the wisdom of the centuries
(In paperback and Kindle format)

Available from Amazon Worldwide

***

Access to videos, podcasts, details of books and much more at:
https://simplicity-in-silence.blogspot.com/

First published in Great Britain 2020
by Brian Holley
Second edition 2021 by Shraddha Books

ISBN 978-1-9196366-0-3

shraddha.books.uk@gmail.com

***

Front Cover: People vector created by renata.s - www.freepik.com
Designed with the help of Jack Andrews

To my sister, Marilyn, whose loving and sincere question started me writing this book.

To my wife, Liz, whose challenging comments and editorial skills have polished this work far beyond my unaided capabilities.

To Tim Ward, whose sympathetic guidance and encouragement helped shape the book.

The God I Left Behind

A journey from fundamentalism to faith

Contents

The God I Left Behind

A journey from fundamentalism to faith

Foreword

My childhood home stood not far from a North Somerset moorland inhabited by large flocks of plover and geese; a place where swans gathered in the winter, where herons fished and voles plied the clear, still water of what we called 'reens' but which was written down as 'rhynes'. The moorlands reached all the way down to the sea shore several miles away, from where I could see the misty otherness of Wales. So my horizons were always far off, beckoning me to adventure. As a child I was often by myself a mile or two from home, content to be among the quiet mysteries of my surroundings. My poor mother would equally often be frantic with worry, having little idea of where to begin looking for me. But I always found my way back to the warmth and security of home.

Maybe it was these experiences that conditioned my attitude to my interior life. I was ever thirsting for something else, something beyond the horizon of my current experience. My subsequent spiritual journey took me, at times, through treacherous and wild places. At other times I walked along beguiling roads, which, I discovered, could be equally treacherous. But eventually, I found myself travelling in a great company of the wise: Buddha, Gandhi, Jesus and Krishna, Jung, Campbell and St. Theresa, Laurens Van der Post and Meister Eckhart, Rumi, Julian of Norwich, Lao Tzu and many more. Although they held such diverse views, they didn't seem to me to be incompatible with one another. In each of their voices I learned to recognise one voice—a still, small voice.

One day, walking with my sister beside Lake Cayuga in upstate New York, she asked me, 'Bri, where are you with God?' I mumbled something incoherent but the question hung over me for the rest of that visit. When I got home to the U.K. I wrote a 2000 word answer but that seemed quite inadequate and I set about something more ambitious than anything I'd ever written before. It is sometimes important to process the past as a means of healing and this is an opportunity for me to do so. This book is about my journey, including the deconstruction of my old faith.

Notes on the Second Edition

It's been seven years since I wrote The God I Left Behind and much has happened in my life since then. For a start, I'm even less religious than I was then, so I might not now express some of the ideas in this book in the same terms. However, the second edition only has minor changes—primarily to do with formatting—but there are a few snippets of additional information that I've added because I thought they would be helpful.

The shedding continues and the inner experience becomes richer. Things I only had a glimmer of a few years back are now becoming clearer. I sincerely hope that this will be the case for you because the only reason for publishing this book is to help others find their own path to whatever it is we think of as Enlightenment.

Weobley
September 2021

PART I

The Making of a Fundamentalist

Krishna went into the forest at night to dance beside the fires with the village girls. When a girl thought in her mind, 'He's all mine', Krishna would disappear.

Hindu myth.

NOTE 1: *This is a tale of two selves: false self and True Self. These terms are used by psychologists and spiritual gurus alike, but not all of their users think of them in the same way, so it will be helpful to begin by illustrating what I mean:*

Part I is the story of the evolution of my ego and my ego's false self. Although the ego doesn't exist as an entity (you can't perform an ego-ectomy) I think of the ego as that aspect of the human mind which gives me a sense of self. It does this largely by discerning the relationship I have with other people and things, and differentiating between them according to how I feel about each relationship—good or bad, superior, inferior or equal. It seems to perform its function largely through the faculties of instinct, memory and imagination, and for most of my life I've been unconscious of how powerful an influence it has had on me.

My false sense of self arises from the colouration given to those discernments and discriminations by my life experiences filtered through natural instincts, inherited traits, culture, education and upbringing. Some people identify this as ego, but I think ego is simply the causing factor. It has an essential job in differentiating between things, and understanding relationships and effects. The false self skews this function leading me to try to be what I'm not and often trying to do that for which I'm unsuited. Psychologists might refer to the false self as the persona but the persona is what helps other people recognise me. It may be laced with false self elements, but as I become more integrated as a human being, this becomes less so—or at least, from my own experience, I become more conscious of this interlacing and am able to handle it.

Between psychologists and spiritual teachers there is considerable confusion about the term 'True Self'. Psychologists use the term to describe the authentic self; generally that is the persona that emerges from one who is self-aware and coping well with life. Some might refer to this as emotional intelligence. For most of us the authentic self, as psychologist Donald Winnicot put it, remains 'concealed, only a virtual possibility.'

But for the spiritual teachers the True Self is at a deeper level than this. It is that within me which is not caught up in the deceptions, projections and blindness of the false self. This is an experience of 'being' rather than in 'doing'. The True Self is that within me which is able to observe the behaviour of the false self. Mystics describe a profound experience of the True Self as Light, the Buddha self, the Christ within, the Atman, the soul, the Self, the Witness, Brahman, the spirit, the Tao or pure consciousness. Ultimately it is a well-spring of peace, love and joy, available to all. It is not an individual aspect of me, but a universal aspect of every being and everything.

Although there are references to 'false self' and 'True Self' throughout the book, I explain them as fully as I am able in Part III.

NOTE 2: *This book contains information about my own experience of Christianity. Although, from many conversations I've had, I find it contains similarities to the experiences of a lot of people, it is unique and should not be regarded as the general experience of all Christians—not even of fundamentalist Christians.*

Chapter One

Father of the Man

Our lives are full of little fictions but, since we live with them from the moment we can understand words, they seem real. Such fictions as dates, times and the highway code become so much a part of our daily lives, we never think of them as being anything other than facts. Yet they are simply fictions people have made up so we can order our lives together, and there's nothing wrong with that. But the greatest fiction of all, and the one least spoken about, so I discovered, is the one about who I am. We refer to it as the persona, a word which originally referred to the mask through which Greek actors spoke—'per sono'. Now we use it to describe how we project our personality to others. It's not the True Self, but the one I want others to think I am; just one more fiction among all the other little fictions, and there's nothing wrong with that either. However, many of my problems arose, as they do for most people, because I thought my persona was who I really am. But this was my ego's 'false self', which had evolved out of seemingly trivial events, and the seeds from which it grew were sown even before I was born.

***

Onward Christian Pea Shooters

Neither of my paternal grandparents had been very committed to religion. Although Gran attended services regularly, Grandpa would attend only if they were going to sing "Onward Christian Soldiers". As a boy my Dad was in the choir, so was able to provide his father with advanced warning if his favourite hymn was on the menu for the following Sunday. To the temporary delight of the vicar, Grandpa would appear, dressed uncomfortably in his best suit.

My maternal grandparents, on the other hand, were committed Congregationalists, yet Mum never spoke about her faith or any spiritual experience she may have had. She attended church regularly and sometimes read the Bible at home, but apart from helping me say bedtime prayers when I was tiny, that was all I ever knew about my mother's religious tendencies.

Dad's experience of church seemed to me much more exciting than Mum's. One of his fellow choirboys would sabotage the organ by putting a loop of string around the redundant pump handle. As the choir came down the aisle in solemn procession, the organ would suddenly run out of air and all that could be heard was the choir's barely repressed giggles of delight. During the sermon some boys surreptitiously aimed their pea-shooters at the vicar's bald head. The congregation must have imagined the poor man was being plagued by insects because he kept slapping the back of his neck, yet never reprimanded them. All this made church sound like fun—not like my experience of boredom and physical discomfort. I gathered from these tales that Dad didn't take his religion very seriously. In my early childhood he was happy to tag along to church with his in-laws. So my parents and grandparents, churchgoers though they were, don't appear to have had much direct influence on what I eventually believed. They never drummed religion into me and so, like most people of my generation, I picked up my religion through a combination of osmosis and Sunday School.

Samoyeds and Smelly Churches

Throughout the Second World War I spent my infancy in my grandparents' house with my parents, my bachelor great-uncle Ernie, who bred Samoyed dogs and, from time to time, my aunt and uncle, when they were on leave from the R.A.F. To this chaotic crowd was added, one February night, my baby sister, who was born in the bedroom next to mine. I hadn't even been aware my mother had been pregnant—one didn't speak of such things in front of the children—so Marilyn's arrival was a bit of a surprise.

On Sunday mornings there was much preening in front of mirrors and complaints about dog-hairs getting on clothes. I added to the Sunday morning chaos by whining, 'Aw, must I go?' and 'It's so boring!' This would make my mother, who was by then already pretty hyper, really cross.

'You're going to church,' she'd snap, and I knew better than to say anything further about the matter. Patience certainly wasn't her strength, especially on Sundays. It was up to Dad, an altogether more gentle personality, to try to calm things down. With a quiet voice he'd persuade me I couldn't stay at home alone, and no, it wouldn't be OK if the dogs looked after me, and he knew I'd be a good boy and not touch anything, but I was going to have to go to church like everyone else.

Grandpa would set off early, as he was a deacon and had to help prepare the church for the service. At 10.30 sharp the narrow hall of Gran and Grandpa's Victorian end-of-terrace house would be filled with people in posh clothes. Like flotsam I was carried along with this tide of adult bodies, out of the door, through the front gate and up the long hill to church. In those wartime days no one in the family owned a car, so we walked everywhere or went by bus. Sadly, buses on Sundays were in as short supply as butter and eggs. I could have wished the family were Baptists, since their church was just around the corner, or even Anglicans, because we passed two of their churches on the way. But at least religion gave us one thing—stamina!

I was made to feel the church building was very holy. It was to me a dark and solemn place with lots of polished wood and brass. My nose was assailed by a concoction of smells, which seemed to consist of damp, polish, flowers, moth-balls, face powder, sweat and breath. The church was such a holy place that people were hushed to silence as they went in. If they found it necessary to say anything, they did so in hoarse whispers. I was afraid even to cough.

Having found our seats, we all bowed our heads in prayer, and then waited for the service to begin. This consisted of the traditional triple sandwich of hymn, prayer and Bible reading, with a big dollop of sermon at the end—just when you were full already. Then it was home to Sunday lunch, prepared earlier in the day by my grandmother, who was an excellent cook. After lunch the menfolk sat in the lounge reading newspapers until sleep overcame them, while the womenfolk cleared up after the meal. I was allowed to play with my toys, but I couldn't go out because I had my Sunday-best clothes on.

With only a brief respite, I headed back up the hill with my mother to Sunday School, where I had to suffer the attention of my Sunday School teacher, an elderly lady with bad breath, who liked to cuddle me. It was a relief to head back once again down the hill for tea. But the relief was short-lived, for after tea the entire family traipsed back to church for the six o'clock service. I can't say the hard pews and long, boring services influenced me spiritually in any way whatsoever. On the other hand the discomfort didn't put me off religion. As a child, I simply accepted it as a fact of life.

School of Hard Knocks

At our temporary home in the Somerset town of Clevedon I experienced a deep sense of security, being surrounded with an extended family of loving adults and three, sometimes four, large Samoyed dogs. Then, when I was six and my sister two, our parents moved us to a house with a large garden in the nearby village of Claverham. Here, I went to Sunday School at the local Methodist church, it being the nearest Nonconformist chapel equivalent to the Congregationalists, and not as far away as the Anglican Church. (We had nothing to do with Roman Catholics.) The Methodist Chapel was a simple building. It had cream distempered walls, long clear windows and old pews, the varnish of which had become dull with age. It was light and simple, unlike the Congregational building—but it still smelled of church.

My memories of my life at Claverham are largely good, but there was a shadow. It began to hover over me at my junior school at Yatton, when I discovered that not all adults were benign–not even teachers.

Within a short time of my arrival I witnessed my first-year teacher lose her temper with a child and rap her knuckles with a side of a wooden ruler. This teacher's method of disciplining infants was terror and it laid a foundation of fear which would play a dominant rôle in my life.

Fortunately I'd arrived at the school late in the school year, so my experience of this particular demon was short.

For the next school year my teacher was everything a teacher should be—kind, firm and inspirational. It was from Mrs. Maslin that I got my lifelong passion for history, but the shadow of fear was not far away. The school hall was divided in two by a folding screen, which had panels of wood in its lower third and glass panels above. My classroom was on one side of the screen, the headmaster's on the other. The activities in the headmaster's class next door could be clearly heard, especially when he lost his temper, which might be several times a day. He had earned the nickname 'Boner', because when he became angry, his face would contort with rage, going bright red, and the bones (more probably veins) in his bald head would stand out. It was a fearsome sight, which, in combination with the angry sounds, induced such terror in me I would usually feel sick on arrival at school. Several times I had to be taken out of assembly into the school yard for some fresh air but, since the air was often freezing cold, this wasn't always the relief it should have been.

Although home was a secure place, despite the difficulties my parents had with health and making ends meet, school was anything but secure. My penultimate junior year was spent under the tutelage of the headmaster's wife, who also had a reputation for severe strictness. I was relieved to discover she was more supportive than I had expected her to be, and this was especially so when she discovered I had some talent in written English. That year went by quickly and the time for me to go into the lion's den - the headmaster's class.

I was not in the A group, his favourites, whom he called by their first names, but in the B group, whom he called by our surnames. Maybe he thought we needed more driving; he certainly knew nothing about leading. I was glad I wasn't in the C group though. He looked down on these children because they would never pass the 11 plus exam, and he regarded them as irredeemable failures. It was these poor souls who were usually the butt of his sarcasm and anger, and at whom I'd heard him yelling for the previous two years.

An Early Awakening

One night, during this difficult period, I had a strange experience. Though I was tucked snugly into my warm bed, I was ruminating on the terrors I might have to face the next day. Then something within led me to understand that whatever my bullying headmaster did, there was a part of me he could not touch. In that moment I recognised what I'd later discover Thomas Merton called the 'True Self '– an aspect of me that John O'Donohue said could 'never be wounded'—and I was comforted. In that moment I realised there was nothing my headmaster could say or do to my mind or body which could affect this part of me. From having been awake worrying, I fell into a blissful sleep and from that night on was able to cope reasonably well with the terrors my headmaster inflicted on me and my fellow pupils.

There was one other occasion during this period of my childhood when something even more significantly spiritual happened to me. Late one afternoon during the long summer holiday, I was sitting on the pavement, leaning against a sun-warmed wall. In those days, cars didn't frequent the narrow roads that wound their way through the village, so all was quiet. Where the other village children were I didn't know - probably in the playing field behind the council estate. Neither do I know how long I sat there because, for me, time stood still. Many years later I read something Laurie Lee wrote: 'Never had I felt so fat with time; so free of the need to be doing.'[1] When my eyes fell on those words the memory of my childhood experience flooded back and I knew precisely what he meant. On that village pavement I felt no need to think or do, but just to sit, filled with warm, quiet joy. It seems now to have been a moment of pure enlightenment, an all-too brief window into another state of consciousness, and it arrived unasked for and unexpected, out of sheer grace, as such experiences often seem to do.

1 When I Walked Out One Midsummer Morning, Laurie Lee

Survival of the Fittest

Not that I was a melancholic child or prone to dreaming. I was adventurous and threw myself at life with great enthusiasm, though not always with much thought. By the age of ten I had cut my arm open by breaking a window with my fist and had to have several stitches; been rescued from drowning; shut my finger in the front gate and had a finger nail removed; fallen in a ditch and arrived home covered in tadpoles; stepped in a wasp-nest and arrived home covered in stings; cut my scalp open, front to back on barbed wire and arrived home covered in blood; got stuck in a tunnel I'd tug and got home covered in earth. I'd been knocked off my bike by a car and, without telling my Mum, I cycled four miles across the moors on my sister's tricycle and, later, twelve miles to Bristol on my own bike. Besides all this, on separate occasions, I broke my right forearm and my left elbow. I had more experience of doctors' surgeries and hospital interiors than anyone else I knew!

My natural confidence and experience of being free to roam the countryside made me self-reliant and independent—some called it 'mischievous'. Certainly I had a lot of fun but there was always a serious side to me. I made a puppet theatre and wrote plays for my cardboard characters. A neighbour who was a retired teacher gave me some old text books and I loved looking things up in a massive tome of an encyclopaedia. There were also several books on languages and from them I learned to count to ten in French, German, Hindi, Welsh and Japanese—not exactly useful. It would be more than fifty years before I met a Japanese person to impress with my knowledge of her language.

Home, though secure, was not a place in which I recollect being helped to think about the wider implications of life. My mother wasn't a deep thinker and although my father was, as he proved in later life, he had left school at 13 and was not widely-read. He was a practical man and taught me how to make a crystal set, a one-valve radio and how to fix my bike. He was a keen short-wave listener and we'd be woken in the morning by the sound of a kookaburra from ABC, the Australian Broadcasting Corporation. In the evening, we'd listen to 'Dauncing in Svitzerlant' or

English programmes from Radio Hilversum or Radio Ankara. Dad also liked news programmes in English from Russia and China. The stilted English and the blatant propaganda amused him. But sport from America was his special pleasure, Particularly boxing. As a special treat, I was once allowed to stay up and listen to the 'Big Fight' featuring Joe Louis. But sport was never my thing and I fell asleep before the knock-out.

And so I grew up, exposed to a lot of interesting things but rather naïve. This naïvety often got me into difficult, and sometimes embarrassing situations, such as the time I blurted out something about a 'Jew boy' in the presence of someone whom I later discovered was Jewish. I didn't even understand what a Jew was, let alone that the expression was a serious insult. My naïvety meant I was often caught off balance and this, together with my negative experiences at school, provoked a fearfulness in me that put an anchor on my natural self-confidence. On the one hand, it probably stopped me from being quite as silly as I might have been; on the other it certainly did inhibit my ability to progress my education and career. No doubt my naïvety was a major factor in my eventually becoming a fundamentalist Christian.

Impractical Technicalities

At the end of my last year at Yatton Junior School, I astonished my headmaster by passing my eleven-plus exam, which meant I could go to grammar school where the bright kids went, rather than the Secondary Modern. He immediately began to call me by my first name. My self-esteem had a little growth spurt but the euphoria didn't last long. Just before I was due to start grammar school, my parents moved us to Bristol. I didn't get into the highly competitive Bristol Grammar School, then a Direct Grant school, funded partly by the state and partly by private fees. There were other grammar schools in Bristol but for reasons which, in later life, neither my father nor I understood, I went to a Secondary Modern. I didn't mind. Indeed, I don't recollect being very conscious of what was going on. All my life, adults had made decisions on my behalf without consulting me and I was accustomed to going along with them. That was just the way things were.

I was never an outstanding pupil, except perhaps in English, but I did sufficiently well at Secondary Modern school to be entered for a 13-plus exam and joined a small band of boys who got places at Bristol Secondary Technical School (Engineering). My parents were immensely proud of this achievement but it eventually led me into deeper confusion. Here was a child who, loving English, History and Art, was thrust into a curriculum of physics, mechanics, maths, metalwork, woodwork and technical drawing. I hated almost every minute of it and my constant failures at school began to further erode my natural self-confidence and reinforce my fears. My days were spent fluctuating between the numbness of boredom and gut-wrenching fear because I hadn't done my homework.

Disappointingly Normal

It was around this time that a kindly member of the church sponsored me to go on a Christian holiday at Capernwray Hall in the Lake District. Shortly after arriving in Bristol, I had attended Sunday School at the nearby Plymouth Brethren chapel and eventually graduated to Bible Class. I returned from Capernwray having 'given my heart to Jesus'. The 'great event' happened on the Thursday evening, my having resisted until then the daily invitations of our host. I knew I ought to respond and I was waiting for something to drag me on to my feet and take me to the counselling room. But nothing happened. I suppose, since it was the last but one day of the holiday, I might have thought I'd miss the opportunity if I didn't decide that night, so up I got and went forward. I remember saying a special prayer with the help of one of the leaders, being given a little pamphlet about being a Christian and then feeling disappointed that I didn't feel any different. I'd thought, indeed had been led to believe, that 'giving my heart to Jesus' was going to be some kind of supernatural experience. I had imagined a miraculous change would take place. After all, we'd been singing the old evangelical song all week:

Since Jesus came into my heart,
Since Jesus came into my heart;
Floods of joy o'er my soul like the sea billows roll,
Since Jesus came into my heart.

Such songs certainly raised my expectations and, whereas I didn't expect choirs of angels to break forth in hallelujahs, or doves to descend, floods of joy would have been OK. Whatever I had expected, I really didn't expect to feel—normal. After all, having Jesus in your heart would, I thought, be big-time compared to just going to Bible class. Those who heard of my commitment gushed with encouragement but for me there were still no floods of joy—not even a trickle! I tried to respond positively to their obvious delight but inside my emotional pool was dry. I guess my ego's false self was desperately trying to find comfort by being part of the crowd I happened to find myself with. I later learned this is normal false self behaviour.

By Saturday morning, I still felt normal. Indeed, when I looked in the mirror I even looked normal, and this awful feeling of normality remained with me all the way home. However, my kindly sponsor seemed overjoyed when he got news of my 'conversion'. Shortly after our return, those of us who had been on the holiday were invited to tea at his big house in Pembroke Road. When this genial man, a world-renowned surgeon, put his large hand on my shoulder and told me how pleased he was that I had given my heart to Jesus, I felt a bit guilty. Some instinct within me made me vaguely aware something transcendent should have taken place, and what I'd experienced wasn't 'it'. But I wouldn't have understood the term transcendent at that time; everyone seemed so pleased with me and my ego enjoyed a good grooming, which made me feel very proud and secure.

Perhaps I've inherited a Dawkins God-gene because, undeterred by this experience, a year or so later I went forward at the Billy Graham Crusade at Haringey in London. Now that was a real high. The huge crowd, the music, the exultant singing, Beverley Shay's heart-rending solos, and the authoritative voice of Dr. Graham calling us to get out of our seats and come down, brought tears to my eyes.

Hindsight now shows me I'd got caught up in a loop of psychological energy, generated from the platform, and then amplified in the crowd. It was, no doubt, a more positive version of the phenomenon manifested among crowds in Nuremberg, but technically, it wasn't too different. A fairer comparison might be that experienced regularly by crowds at football clubs and theatres throughout the land. Whereas I recognise some people's lives were profoundly affected by the Billy Graham crusades and others like them, the emotional energy was, in many cases, more to do with the ego than anything spiritual. Egos get so easily caught up in rushes of psychological and emotional energy, especially when it occurs in what Carl Jung called the 'collective ego', and at Haringey there was one big collective ego. But individuals can't sustain that level of hype for long. So for me the euphoria wore off during the long coach journey home and, the next day, I was back to disappointing old normality once again.

A Missing Link?

Looking back at this confusing and insecure period of my life, I realise I probably just wanted to feel that I belonged, something I'd lost since moving away from our country village and all my friends. Subconsciously I wanted to find the real me that grace had introduced me to, albeit briefly, as I leaned against that sun-warmed wall in Claverham. But all I was finding was the unreal me, the religious me, the me that was either what other people wanted me to be, or the one who couldn't become what other people wanted me to be.

Reflecting on my early childhood later in life I became aware that although I can remember holding my father's hand, sitting on his lap and being cuddled by him, I can't remember having the same experience with my mother. When I see little grandsons cuddling into their mums, I sigh inwardly. It wasn't that I ever felt unloved, but I don't remember my mother showing her affection to me as readily as my father did. Considering that, and the unsettled environment we all experienced as a result of war in my first two years, a stage of infancy when stability has been shown to be essential, it is hardly surprising I took a long time to mature.

By my early teens I'd drifted away from the church, and my parents no longer insisted I went with them. It was about this time that Dad became interested in Hindu Yoga through reading books by Paul Brunton. He even got Mum, my sister Marilyn and me practising the lotus position, to our great discomfort. One day, when we got up after such a session, Mum remained sitting. Dad thought she was really getting the idea of it but she complained her legs had become locked in place and she couldn't move! Such contortions were not going to convert us, it seemed, and pictures in Dad's books of yogis with long needles through their cheeks were enough to put off even the most avid yoga enthusiast.

At school I was constantly in trouble for not doing my homework and I always took a lead in playing up weak teachers. Consequently, I was regularly humiliated with punishments. School and fear began to become identified with one another and so, after two years and before taking any exams, I left to get a job. My departure was accompanied by a mixture of relief and a sense of failure. I was the only one in my year to leave early but I was jubilant that I no longer had to study maths and science, and particularly pleased not to have to take part in metal work and wood work classes.

Damaged Cars and Guitars

I had no concept of the kind of person I was and certainly didn't know what I wanted to do. So when the man at the Employment Office suggested that, since I'd had an engineering education and my Dad was a motor mechanic, I should follow him into the motor trade, I acquiesced.

Soon I was crawling around under lorries, helping to replace gearboxes, radiators, wheel bearings and back axle parts. I learned about fixing engines and windscreens, door locks and steering mechanisms. I hated it. I hated the dirt, the cold, the diesel fumes and the language of my fellow mechanics. I wasn't the least excited about new models and modifications. While others sat eating their sandwiches and chatting about women and football, I read books on archaeology. Not that I'm inferring there is anything wrong with chatting about women and football—I was certainly interested in the former—it was just that this just wasn't the right place for me. But what did I do? I acquiesced. I joined in with the vulgarity, tried to appear interested in the work and muddled through for a couple of years. But after inflicting several thousand pounds worth of damage on customers' vehicles, I was fired. Once again, I had escaped from a miserable existence doing things I hated. I felt like a prisoner reprieved.

For a year I drifted from one unsatisfactory job to another, but then I found music. My parents had always insisted that I was musical from the day of my Christening. Apparently I had squirmed around vigorously as soon as the organ began to play. However, when my mother put me to the violin at the age of seven, I showed little interest. Locked in the front room to practise, I climbed out of the window and went off with my friends. It would be eight years later, when I heard Italians playing their guitars in a coffee bar that I would be inspired to take up music. I bought a Spanish guitar and began practising in my bedroom. Eventually I joined a Skiffle group as lead singer and when this folded, I started a vocal group called the Sapphires. There were four of us fellows and a girl. We became well known among the clubs and pubs of Bristol, and one year we came first in the then famous 'Carroll Levis Show'. Thus encouraged, in 1959 we turned professional and I felt at last I was about to become somebody.

We moved to London did a tour of military bases with Combined Services Entertainment, did a gig in the Dorchester Hotel, worked in clubs in London and Manchester, and even appeared on television several times. But by the time we returned from a six week summer season, I realised show business was not for me. I had begun to break out in a nervous rash every time we went on stage. We were appearing in a supporting rôle on the BBC Celebrity dais at the Radio Show and staying in a hotel in Earl's Court, when a blazing row broke out. Two of us walked out and so, nine months after leaving home for fame and fortune, I returned home, neither famous nor fortunate.

Throughout this time I neither thought of nor talked of "God", nor had anything whatsoever to do with religion. I felt lonely and isolated but that was nothing very new. My previous experiences of religion hadn't done anything to relieve that pain so there was no point in looking there. I did what I guess most young people do: got on with enjoying life as best I could, which involved quite a lot of beer, girls and music.

Chapter Two

Out of the Frying Pan

Love and the Sergeant Major

I was twenty years old and my life was just a jumble of confusion. I didn't know who I was or what I should do, yet my situation was about to get even worse. Within a month of leaving the group, I was called up for National Service. To my utter frustration, the call came just as I had fallen in love. It was the third time this had happened that year -- falling in love I mean. The first time was just before the group moved to London. The girl and I wrote regularly for a while but absence did not make the heart grow fonder and she faded from memory. The second time was to a girl I met at our summer season venue. She claimed to have been a dancer with Madame Bluebell in Paris, but when I met her at Butlins in Skegness, she was working on the electric shaver kiosk. We had a passionate affair but when she came to visit me in Bristol later, the magic had gone for both of us.

My new girlfriend was from a strict Plymouth Brethren family, which was quite coincidental to my previous connections with a Brethren chapel and my 'conversions'. She brought something into my life I'd been lacking for most of my teens—a sense of belonging and respect. I suppose I found in her something of that motherly affection I seemed to have missed in my childhood.

We didn't meet in church but in a coffee bar, a fact that had to be kept secret from her somewhat austere parents. Indeed, when I visited the family home, I had to be very careful not to use such terms as 'cinema', 'pub', 'pop music' or 'cigarettes' and, if I hurt myself in their presence, to remember not to use any of the words I'd learned while working in the garage.

My impending in-laws turned out to be highly-committed fundamentalist Christians. They didn't have television, didn't drink alcohol or smoke and wouldn't listen to the radio or read newspapers on Sundays. They read the Bible every day, said grace before every meal and went to church more often than there were days in the week, or so it seemed to me. They were good people at heart, and I often wondered what they thought of me. I must have made a reasonably good impression, otherwise I'm sure my girlfriend's father would have told me, quite unambiguously, that I should no longer darken their front gate, let alone their doorstep.

Later I reflected that no aspect of their religious practices seemed to have given my future in-laws any sense of peace. My girlfriend's father was a particularly fearful man, partly, I guess, from an over-strict upbringing and partly because he had spent some forty years in a job he hated. I remember him becoming greatly agitated at my having bought his youngest son some chips when we were out on a Sunday. Such was his anger at my infringement of the Sabbath, he drove us home like a maniac, gripping the steering wheel so firmly his knuckles went white. It should have been my first clue to the fact that Bible-believing religion doesn't necessarily lead to deep spiritual experience, but then I was still deeply unconscious of my own person, let alone spiritual matters.

I arrived at Le Marchant Barracks in Devizes in the back of a draughty army lorry in early November 1959. Basic training in the Army was like nothing I'd ever experienced before. We were billeted in a 'well-ventilated' and poorly-insulated Victorian barracks, and I shared a room with about eleven other lads. There was a coke boiler at one end of the room and I was lucky enough to have a bed only a few feet away. Those at the far end had to put their heavy army greatcoats over their blankets at night to keep warm. It was a cold, grey winter and we weren't allowed out of the barracks for the first three weeks. I was irritated by such confinement and particularly by the corporals and sergeants, whose job it was to hassle us mere civilians into becoming soldiers. It was their job to induce fear in us, so we would respond automatically to orders in the field. Since I was already fearful, this didn't take much to achieve, and I was hurting inside a lot of the time.

Mostly I was hurting from not being with the girl I loved. I felt sick with anticipation at the arrival of the post each morning and depressed all day if a letter from her didn't come. Not that there was much rich content in our letters, just affirmations of love, but that was enough for me. Had I been more mature, I may have better understood the quality of that relationship for, although my feelings were overpoweringly strong, when I ‘phoned my girlfriend two or three times a week, we had little to say to each other. But this time absence was doing its job and when eventually I got home for a weekend, we spent every possible moment silently entwined and oblivious to the world. I was just one big bundle of acute love-sickness.

Within a year we were married and had our first child. I was delighted, and I guess having someone else dependent on me gave my ego's false self a considerable boost, though that clearly wasn't the main cause. As a husband and father I felt I had some status—so much so, that within two years, twins arrived. Now I was in charge of a substantial household, with a home and responsibilities. Although my in-laws were extremely supportive, as were my own parents, and on the surface I appeared to be coping well, inside I was still in a state of turmoil. I was prone to angry outbursts and, to my shame, I'm sure I terrified my wife and the children at times.

Religion, an Oboe and an Ally.

About this time I started to go to Bible classes at the Methodist Church. These were run by a reader from the Soldiers' and Airmen’s Scripture Readers Association (SASRA). I tried hard to find peace through these sessions, but found none. A better option, I found, was to go cycling. I had been a keen cyclist most of my life but hadn't done much since the *Sapphires* had got together. I bought a bike and the exercise helped relieve some of my frustrations.

In desperation for better financial security, I had signed on for a six-year service contract as a regular soldier. By a twist of fate I managed to get into the band. I think, because I had 'professional guitarist' as my civilian occupation, it was assumed I could actually play at that level. In fact I'd only strummed an accompaniment to basic rock-and-roll songs, but my ego's 'false self' had stretched this into something rather more exotic. The bandmaster didn't know this and assumed I'd be able to play with the dance band, but told me I had to learn a second instrument. I said I'd like to try a clarinet.

'Sorry,' said the bandmaster, 'I've got no vacancies on the clarinet, but I do need an oboist.' I had only a vague idea of what an oboe was, but said yes anyway. He gave me an instrument, a box of reeds and a tutor book, and told me to find a quiet place (for example, a loo) and learn it. I became an oboist.

It didn't take me long to discover just how hard it is to blow an oboe, and it took a considerable time to build up an embouchure (the strength of facial muscle) to control the reeds. My poor wife would find something to do in the garden when I practised, for not only was the sound I made uninteresting, consisting largely of scales, it also had yet to develop any sweetness of tone. Worst of all, it was *very* loud. No wonder it has the reputation of being the ill wind that nobody blows any good!

I tried very hard to become proficient with the instrument and had a certain amount of help from a couple of older and more experienced band members. However, although I eventually learned to play with a very modest level of competence and even passed my A2 exam, I was not good at sight-reading and still suffered with nerves when called upon to play solos. Fortunately, I had an ally—the flautist.

He sat next to me and knew my limitations. We never discussed it. He just knew I'd never get my fingers around anything faster than a semi-quaver and played my most difficult cues. The Bandmaster never seemed to notice, so I bluffed my way through my army career and adequately supported my family while not having to indulge in the dirty work of soldiering as a rifleman.

My experience with the dance band was humiliating. I didn't know a lot of the complicated chords demanded by the scores and it soon became apparent I couldn't play the solos either. Nothing was said. After the first two or three practices I wasn't invited to practise with the dance band any more.

However, marching band was fun and for that, fancy dress (blues uniform with red stripes and a white belt) was obligatory. Another bonus was that oboists don't carry their instruments on parade. I suppose a sharp double reed jerking about in your mouth would soon have you bleeding all over your sheet music. Oboists therefore carry cymbals in a marching band. I could manage that.

At the time I could never have admitted my sense of failure to myself, but looking back, I know I experienced a constant nag of dissatisfaction. But there was nothing I could do about it. I had signed on for six years and there was no chance of my being able to afford to buy myself out of that contract. There was nothing for it but to see it through. At least no one seemed anxious to expel me from the band; my family were by then accommodated in a brand new married quarter and I was satisfactorily paid. But there had to be more to life than this.

Chapter Three

Into the Fire

'Irrevocable commitment to any religion is not only intellectual suicide; it is positive unfaith because it closes the mind to any new vision of the world.'
Alan Watts

Dark Days in the Sun

At the end of 1962 our long anticipated posting came through. Rumours had been rife in the regiment for months. It was to be Berlin, Ireland, Malaya or even Yorkshire! Then in December my little family and I packed our boxes, boarded the troop ship *Oxfordshire* and sailed to Malta. The week-long journey and the first couple of months settling in to our new, and to us, exotic location provided a distraction from reality. The excitement of travel and new places to see enabled me to overlay my personal feelings of insecurity with activity, but subconsciously I was dragging behind me a failed education and a whole series of failed jobs, including my present one.

After the short respite of our settling-in period, I woke up to realise I was now not only an unhappy soldier and an unsuccessful musician but I was in a none-too-happy marriage as well. There were also a whole host of people making demands on my life: officers and NCOs, as well as a wife and the babies. I was drowning in a sea of personal unconsciousness and, like anyone drowning, I thrashed around a lot. I'm sure my neighbours in our block of flats in Sliema must have wondered if there was a volcano on the ground floor, for I would erupt fairly regularly with much yelling and slamming of doors. I'd long lost the sense of self I'd encountered, albeit briefly, as a child in the country. Now I didn't know who I was and therefore no one else could know who I was either, including those nearest to me. It's difficult to relate to someone in that condition. If you don't know who you are, you can't expect anyone else to know who you are either!

My sense of isolation followed me like a faithful dog—a black dog. At this point I could see clearly that I wasn't a musician; I was merely musical. I didn't have the hand-to-eye co-ordination necessary to sight-read and move my fingers on the keys with dexterity, as my bandsman colleagues could. Most of those with whom I served had committed themselves long-term to army life. I couldn't do that and yearned passionately for the day I could be free. I despised the petty restrictions and uniformity. The regimental pride, expressed by some long serving soldiers, left me absolutely cold. I respected few of the officers and even fewer of the NCOs—liked some of them, yes; feared others, but I could not find much truly to respect in them. I was an outsider trying to be an insider and probably not fooling anyone—except perhaps myself.

After several months of increasing emotional misery, I reached a depth of darkness I'd never visited before and decided to give religion another chance. I'm still deeply ashamed of the situation that tipped me over the edge into this decision. My wife had gone swimming with friends one evening, while I baby-sat. At ten o'clock my possessive ego considered she should be home and I began fretting. At eleven, I left the kids and walked the hundred yards to the beach to fetch her. I found her in the water frolicking with a couple of our male friends and it made me intensely jealous. I ordered her home and, although I'm sure it was entirely innocent on her part, she having been brought up with two brothers, we had an awful row and I struck her. The guilt of that act seized me and I felt awful for days. Then one evening, I rushed to the bedroom, fell on my knees and told "God", in a most melodramatic way, that if He'd have me, I was coming back. The latter part was all good stuff for testimonies at religious meetings in subsequent years, but, on reflection, such a display was actually just as much a demonstration of my own state of unconsciousness, as the act that seems to have provoked it.

Oh Brother!

We started attending a British Methodist Church just outside Valletta but I found the 'hymn-and-prayer' sandwich routine, rather than satisfying my spiritual hunger, left me feeling empty and cold. Much to the delight of my Plymouth Brethren in-laws, I found a Brethren Gospel Hall secreted in the basement of a tall building in the back streets of Floriana. The only sign of its presence was a small plaque on the wall. As I'd never attended a Brethren morning service before, the meetings were quite a revelation. Everyone sat waiting for the Lord to move someone to announce a hymn, say a prayer or read a passage from the Bible and perhaps expound upon it. Anyone might take part, it seemed, as long as they were male. The Lord didn't move women, except to play the piano or make tea afterwards. Because such an attitude towards women was common in society in those days, it never occurred to me that it was sexist. The church was run on the basis of instructions found in Paul's letters in the New Testament. Therefore men kept their heads uncovered and could take part in the service. Women wore hats and remained silent (except to sing a hymn, if a man announced one). If visiting women arrived without hats, there was a collection of millinery in the spare room they could choose from. I noticed that women visitors who had experienced this kind gesture rarely returned.

Being a Christian had a positive effect on my relationship with my wife and the family. I was much less frustrated and our flat became a home from home for a number of my comrades-in-arms. I began to feel better about myself, though there was always an underlying personal dissatisfaction that tended to blight everything. I could never achieve the level of morality I imagined I should attain as a Christian and so there hung over me a pall of guilt, which no amount of praying could completely eliminate.

No one ever referred to the church as 'fundamentalist', yet the teaching I received from the good brothers of the Gospel Hall was undoubtedly of that brand of Christianity. It was many years before I discovered that the term 'fundamentalist' had arisen in the opening years of the 20th Century. By that time many Christians were becoming alarmed by the rise of liberalism in the church. They were greatly offended by the discoveries of Charles Darwin and other scientists, and by textual and archaeological research that was throwing new light on the origins of the Bible. The first recorded use of the term was at the Niagara Bible Conference late in the 19th century and it broke into the religious vocabulary in 1910, through a meeting of the General Assembly of the Presbyterian Church. This meeting established that certain Christian doctrines were immutable: the inerrancy of the Bible, the doctrine that the Bible contained everything necessary to salvation, that Jesus was born of a virgin, that He died on the Cross as a sacrifice for the sins of mankind, that He arose from the dead and would soon return from heaven to rule over the earth. It was a package. If Christians deviated from these fundamentals, they were at best, heretics, at worst, damned. I became 'orthodox'.

My wife was pleased to be on familiar ground with the Brethren Church and her parents were positively ecstatic at my conversion and commitment to the Gospel Hall. So much so, they made their first and, I believe, only journey by air to visit us.

Evangelists, Spies and Politicians

One day an American evangelist named Ray turned up 'out of the blue' at our meeting. He'd come in on the ferry from Sicily with exciting stories of 'living by faith'. Someone commented that his was a 'hand to mouth existence'. Ray agreed, but said it was from God's hand to his mouth. He travelled 'as he felt moved by the Lord'. So, having spent some weeks in Sicily, he headed for the jetty, feeling a call to visit Malta. The only snag was that he had no money. Nevertheless, he believed the Lord would provide and, it seems, He did. For just as the ferry was about to leave, one of Ray's Sicilian friends turned up and gave him some money. He told many such stories, which made an enormous impression on me at the time.

Ray stayed at our apartment. It was, for us, a service to "God". He and I travelled around the island cornering unsuspecting Maltese, drawing them into conversation and trying to convert them from their 'evil' Roman Catholic beliefs. I remember two young men we'd been 'ministering to' at the docks at Valletta. We had promised to talk again and when we turned up a few days later, I spotted them falling over one another trying to hide behind some barrels. Undeterred, Ray marched up to the barrels, leaned over to the cowering couple and tried to engage them in conversation.

'The priest told us we mustn't to speak to you,' they said.

'If, after you die, you discover at the Judgement Throne you've been wrong in your beliefs, what would you do?' Ray asked.

One of the lads replied, 'We'd say we did what the priest told us to and so it would be the priest's fault, not ours.' There being no way to counter this, we prayerfully left them to their fate.

One day we had a meeting with the, then, aspiring prime minister of Malta, Dom Mintoff. He was very happy to welcome us into his home and talk about the possibility of setting up a Christian radio station on the island. I felt very important to be carrying out the Lord's work at this level of society. It was contact with Mr. Mintoff that eventually led us into a situation involving the security services, though it was perfectly innocent as far as we were concerned.

My brush with the leader of Malta's Labour Party and my consequent feelings of importance acted rather like an analgesic. It gave temporary relief from some of the pain that came from knowing I was in the wrong job. The job wasn't important, I reasoned. "God" had led me here to convert Maltese people to true faith in Jesus. If I ran into difficulty, I knew it to be God's will because everything was His will. Maybe he was testing me or preparing me for some great work. So, not only did I praise "God" when things went well, I praised him when things got difficult as well. A new cliché entered my vocabulary: 'Hallelujah, anyway!'

Quite suddenly and unexpectedly Ray received a 'call from God' to move on. The last I heard of him he was in India deliberating whether it should be an act of faith to drink the local water without boiling it first. In my reply, I urged him to use common sense. After all Paul recommended Timothy to drink wine 'for his stomach's sake' and his frequent illnesses.

Sunday, of course, was our big day. There was a meeting and Sunday School in the morning. Some of the ladies would take it in turns to run the Sunday School. My family would return home to share lunch with a crowd of fellow soldiers. After lunch and a trip to the beach, we'd all have tea before catching the bus to Floriana in time for the evening meeting. I often took my guitar to this meeting to accompany the singing of Christian songs, some of which I'd written. Church was beginning to feel like fun.

The Sunday evening Gospel meeting was an opportunity for the good news of salvation through Jesus to be preached to unbelievers, even though I can only remember two unbelievers ever attending. On arrival they were greeted and, as was customary, the hatless female was asked to cover her head choosing from the collection of hats on offer from the store cupboard. These had been donated inevitably by elderly members of the church, so none of them were likely to go well with the neat pale blue suit which the young lady was wearing. Eventually we discovered that these two were actually Special Branch spies, sent to investigate us when Dom Mintoff's Labour Party Press printed some tracts for us containing anti-Catholic propaganda. We had distributed them throughout Valletta and Sliema just before a sensitive election. Mr. Mintoff clearly had a different agenda from ours. Our motive was to save the poor Maltese people from the clutches of the 'Beast' (the Roman Catholic Church, in our view). Mr. Mintoff just wanted to diminish the influence of the church over the politics of the island. He was hoping for a better chance of winning the election. At that time the Maltese church owned a substantial amount of property on the Islands for which it paid no local taxes. Our understanding was that Dom Mintoff had promised to redress this injustice if he was elected, and this was a threat to the church authorities, who had strongly influenced previous elections against him. But the political implications of our action didn't come to our attention until we serving soldiers were called upon to put on our best uniforms and 'bulled' boots, and appear in front of our respective commanding officers. They reprimanded us—in the nicest possible way—for having become embroiled in local politics. Thereafter, the nice young couple never again came to the Gospel Hall. I imagine this was not one of their most challenging spying missions and often wondered if, in their report, they ever mentioned the hat!

Fundamentalism can lead to all sorts of difficult choices. One Sunday morning an elder found he didn't have enough fuel to drive to church.

Instead of buying petrol on a Sunday, which would have broken the Sabbath, he caught a bus. On later reflection I realised that, like all of us, he actually lived more than a Sabbath day's journey from church, but I wouldn't have liked to have been the one to tell him that.

Man with a Mission

In being part of the church's collective ego I discovered a sense of security, which had been missing for much of my life. My religious enthusiasm was warmly acceptable to the experienced elders and, supported by 'readers' from SASRA, my friends and I became missionaries in our barracks.

In those days, I had all my theology worked out from Bible commentaries and books of a certain kind. It was all stored neatly in my brain in the psychological equivalent of box files. If it was a question of creation, original sin, redemption, resurrection, the end of the world, judgement or the Bible, all relevant theology, with supporting verses, could be retrieved in neat bundles of clichés. Thus I hoped to confound those who argued against the One Truth. Life inside my religion was certain. It was only uncertain in the world beyond, but then the Bible and the church told me to expect that. The Devil was on the prowl 'like a hungry lion', said St. Paul, and all opposition to my point of view I deemed to be the Devil's prowling. All I needed to do was stick to the script, like everyone else, and all would be well.

The script was the Bible and certain 'reliable' commentaries, which I devoured like a starving man. Indeed, many years later, I discovered I was indeed starving, intellectually at least, and it was largely my intellectual hunger I was really satisfying. I was into mind-stuff, right up to my neck —or should that be 'scalp'? But spirituality is like water, it finds its way into the 'soul' in the most unlikely ways—perhaps like rain through a leaking roof - or, as Leonard Cohen sang, 'Everything has a crack in it. That's how the light gets in.' Even during this time of emotional instability and intellectual poverty, I was able to experience a measure of spiritual sustenance, though I don't think I identified it as such at the time. In those days I thought religion and spirituality were the same thing, and it would be many years before I experienced spirituality neat, without the need of a religious mixer.

However, I had reached a place where at last I could enjoy some sense of self-identity. I would eventually discover that a self-identity obtained through religion may be no more truly 'me', than one derived from being a motor mechanic, a shop assistant, a soldier or a musician, but for now it was enough. In those days my beliefs were the most important thing in my life and I became seriously uncomfortable when people challenged them. I now see clearly how much my self-identity was tied to those beliefs. To attack my beliefs, was to attack me. The 'true self' doesn't experience such problems because it knows self-identity is nothing to do with beliefs, opinions, doctrines or membership, but rests on a palpable experience of 'who I truly am'. My response to challenges was to project my fears back on to my antagonists and derive the satisfaction of believing they would eventually have to face judgement and the wrath of "God". There was a sad incident that illustrates this. My family and I returned to England at the end of 1965, and my parents met us at R.A.F. Lyneham. My wife, five-year-old daughter and three-year-old twins piled into the back of the car with my mother, while I sat in the front beside Dad. Not long into the journey, I began to try to convert my parents to my brand of Christianity. When they politely declined, I felt hurt and angry that my message hadn't got through and told them quite plainly that they would suffer in Hell for eternity. Years later, we could laugh together about that awful journey but, at the time, I'd got religion and I'd got it bad!

Turned on to Jesus

I left the Army in 1966, after a short posting in Germany, and just before the birth of our fourth child. I quickly got a job in a personnel department and became involved with our nearest Gospel Hall at Lawrence Weston, a suburb to the north of Bristol. For the first time I felt fulfilled at work and liberated, now I was free of the Army. During the first three months after my discharge, I felt I was walking on air all day and every day. But at night I was tortured by a recurring nightmare. I was standing before my

Commanding Officer being told I'd not handed in my notice to leave the army in time, and was not being allowed to go. I'd wake up sweating.

Then some new developments in religion began to excite me—even though they terrified the older members of our church. The cultural revolution of the 60s, with its more liberal attitudes expressed primarily in rock and roll, promiscuity, drugs and political protest, was beginning to find its way into religion. However, rather than 'liberating' religion, it was tending to drive some towards fundamentalism, albeit of a more exciting, even flamboyant kind.

American evangelists were coming to the U.K. and addressing large congregations of enthusiastic believers about how they had been getting hippies to 'turn on to Jesus'. Religious rock music was gaining in popularity; I even played guitar in a rock musical put on by an American team in Bristol's Hippodrome Theatre. I was getting that old emotional high again. However, the elders of my church didn't feel the stirrings at all. Indeed, they were very much against any change whatsoever. A friend who left the church then said it was because he could 'no longer conform to their non-conformity'.

Once, I led a small deputation of younger members to address the question of whether it was a true 'leading of the spirit' for Brother Smythe always to announce a hymn at the beginning of morning worship. The elders conferred and agreed it probably wasn't. They approached the brother in question, who received the criticism with good grace. At the next meeting we sat in silence for an abnormally long time. It seemed nobody knew how to begin the meeting! I learned then that orthodoxy doesn't have to be written down.

Paradigm Shift

This kind of behaviour is a living demonstration of what Thomas Kuhn called "a paradigm"[2] and is common throughout all aspects of society. Kuhn worked mainly with scientists who, throughout history, repeatedly found that some well-established theories ran into dead ends as a result of

2 The Structure of Scientific Revolutions, Thomas Kuhn, 1962

new discoveries. Instead of re-evaluating the old theories, scientists tended first to try to deal with the new situation, either by rejecting the new discovery ("if our theory is correct, this discovery isn't possible") or by trying to accommodate the new theory together with the old one. A paradigm was reached because, in scientists' minds, everything had to be evaluated against what had gone before. Even the great Einstein himself once falsified some of his findings to bring them in line with what he thought they should be. Stuck with his own paradigm he couldn't bring himself to believe that the emerging evidence about quantum physics was correct. To those so locked in to the past, change is almost impossible and can only happen to the extent it fits in with expectations derived from previous experience. But among fundamentalist Christians, as I imagine it is with fundamentalists of any persuasion, this is even more true. When you support your case with a "God" who can do anything he likes in any way he wants to, even if it seems illogical and against the laws of nature, there is no objection that will be acceptable to the believer. All things are possible, when you have a god like that.

Kuhn showed the change of mind required to make a 'paradigm shift' was not just confined to a particular issue, but had to be a more general attitude. People had to be open to change on a wide front. If this is difficult for scientists, you can imagine how difficult it is for religious people. No wonder Jesus spoke of the shift in thinking needed as being 'born again' and, for some, it was more difficult than getting a camel through the eye of a needle. I eventually learned that 'paradigmatic' thinking is one of the key characteristics of the ego's 'false self'. Of course, I didn't know anything about "paradigms" then, or the ego, but just around the corner was a paradigm shift of my own.

Chapter Four

Even more fire

As a member of a 'New Testament church' I'd developed a pretty good understanding of the New Testament—though from a very narrow theological perspective. I even attended part-time extra-mural classes at the University of Bristol to learn Koine Greek, the lingua franca of the New Testament writers. I wanted to get closer to what I considered to be 'The Truth' (always with a capital 'T').

According to the New Testament, believers would have various supernatural experiences, such as speaking in tongues, prophesying, seeing mystic visions and healing. I asked an elder why we didn't experience these 'gifts of the spirit' now and he explained that the age of miracles was only to Laonch Christianity—a sort of religious loss-leader I suppose. He referred me to a passage in 1 Corinthians in which Paul says such things would cease[3]. The answer didn't satisfy me one bit. Paul was talking about the end times and we weren't there yet. Then I asked a Brethren evangelist, 'What do you think about speaking in tongues?' He simply grinned, looked at me sideways and said, 'Hallelujah'. I was mildly shocked, but took it that such an experience was actually OK among some parts of the church. Therefore, being the Ego-driven young man that I was, I plunged headlong into the Charismatic movement. This was a level of fundamentalism even the original fundamentalists hadn't thought about.

A question I asked one of the visiting American evangelists showed how conservatively fundamentalist I'd become. He'd been a jazz musician before he'd 'found Jesus' and I asked him if he thought it was OK for me, as a believer, to listen to jazz and pop music or should I only listen to religious music. He sensibly answered that any music was OK.

Ego is Ego—Religious or Not!

By this time we had bought our first home and I set out to evangelise the neighbourhood. As part of this programme I invited local children off the

3 I Corinthians 13:8

housing estate to our home for a club evening. This went well and soon our little living room was crammed with children every Tuesday evening. We played games with them and they listened to religious stories told by candlelight. It was at this point that I met a Pentecostal couple who, unknown to me, owned a church on the estate. They had personally purchased a redundant chapel, decorated it and, with another couple, opened it to all. Unfortunately, those who did come didn't continue to come and this valiant foursome battled on fruitlessly for some years. When they discovered me and my children's club they were anxious to join forces. They offered me their premises for a Sunday school and the use of a small minibus to collect and deliver kids from the area. I got caught up in this, believing "God" was calling me to something great and never asking why they had had to finance everything themselves or why no one else ever attended their services. My ego's false self identified itself as a spiritual hero that would rescue the church and become a source of spiritual health for the somewhat run down community on the estate. I had not discerned that the couple had serious mental health issues and it took a couple of years before these began to manifest themselves.

Once I became aware of what was going on I withdrew from the church and was assailed by accusations and threats. I was accused of stealing Sunday School money and of damaging the van. Worse, when one of the other partners in the project died suddenly of a heart attack, I was blamed for causing him so much stress. The dominant wife of the partnership came to our house and threatened me on several occasions. When we refused to answer the door she would scream abuse through the letterbox. Then came a solicitor's letter threatening to sue me. I went to see the solicitor to explain the situation. He said little but his body language told me all I needed to know. He reassured me that he didn't expect the matter to go any further. I wish someone could have been there to explain the operation of the false self to me for, with hindsight, this had been a purely ego experience from beginning to end. I learned much from it later in life but at the time I was just sore. Eventually the attacks subsided and we began visiting a charismatic house church on the other side of town.

Fire Descends

My new charismatic friends told me I should ask "God" to baptise me in the spirit. I'd already been baptised in the sea in Malta but this was something quite different. Baptism in the spirit, it seemed, was to be the overwhelming experience I'd expected as a young boy at Capernwray Hall and at the Earl's Court crusade. I sought the experience for a long time with no success. Then one day it came upon me at a most unexpected and perhaps even inconvenient moment.

I had been meeting for prayer regularly with a Pentecostal friend in an Anglican Church near my office—usually during our lunch breaks. We'd lay our 'shopping lists' of requirements before "God" in a small chapel at the entrance to the church. Then, one day, I suddenly felt overwhelmed by an ecstasy of love and began to babble word-like sounds which seemed to give expression to the love I felt. Quite involuntarily, it seemed, I was speaking in tongues. Every fibre of my body glowed and I guess the nearest I can get to a description isn't very religious. It was the biggest and best orgasm I'd ever had. Tears coursed down my face and it took some time before I could recover enough decorum to leave the church and return to my office. I went back to work walking on air, and continued to feel such elevation for some days afterwards. It was a strange experience, all the more so because, like my mini-enlightenment experience at the age of nine, it had come 'out of the blue'. My consciousness seemed to have expanded and for a while everything was brighter and more in focus.

I now prefer to reserve judgement on what this experience actually was, because I can still speak in tongues. Maybe, once experienced, it's something you can always do—like riding a bike. Although I don't believe it to be a supernatural event, generated from something outside of myself, I'm nevertheless happy to consider it to be a spiritual one. I once read that, by using brain-scanning technology at the Center for Spirituality and the Mind at the University of Pennsylvania, it was found when people speak in tongues there is a drop in frontal lobe activity and normal language centres are not in operation. Their conclusions were that the phenomenon is not the product of normal decision-making and, although tongues are not identifiable as actual language, those who exercise the 'gift' are not making up the words from their imagination—they're not faking it. Certainly I still find speaking in tongues to be quite effortless and often to be accompanied by that now familiar sense of peace, love and joy which I regard as the 'fruits of the spirit'. Tongues, or glossolalia if you want to be technical, seem to give expression to a heightened consciousness of love in a way normal language can't always achieve.

A Passionate Pursuit

After this experience I read the Bible before breakfast, and again on the bus to work. I stepped up the time I spent in praying in my lunch breaks and attended worship meetings, prayer meetings and gospel meetings. If there was a gathering of my fellow believers, I'd be there. I became a lay preacher on a small non-conformist circuit in North Bristol, probably frightening the lives out of the conservative congregations of country folk with my passionate sermons. I was rock-certain of my beliefs in those days. My paradigm was as securely in place as the 'Iron Curtain'. But neither would stand the test of time.

In all this period of my life I never questioned my beliefs and this was not surprising because I was surrounded by enthusiastic people, who affirmed them to be correct. To have faith meant to be certain of my doctrines. Not to be certain of them was to be unfaithful—why, even heretical!

These were the early days of the Charismatic movement; we were all finding our way. It's hardly surprising then, that certain excesses happened, just as they did among Protestants of various sorts in the Reformation period and even more so among Christians of the early church.

One day we were invited by a friend to travel down into Somerset to the town of Chard, where a local farmer held open house on Sundays.

There were perhaps twenty five or thirty people crowded into a barn for a time of praise and worship. There was much speaking in tongues, interpretation of tongues and prophesying, and a woman explained a vision she had had. Someone else asked for healing and a small group, presumably of 'elders', were invited to lay hands on the patient. Each took it in turn to exhort the Lord to 'move upon our sister here' and to 'overcome the work of Satan'. They reminded "God" most fervently of his promises to heal in the New Testament, then turned to the patient and commanded her to get well. I never learned the outcome.

After a shared lunch we were invited to a hay loft, where someone was to have demons cast out of them. To my immature and insecure little mind it was all very exciting, though I must admit to having felt a shadow of unease about the situation. However, by then I'd learned how easy it is to conform to the demands of the collective ego. To have expressed doubts would have brought me more opposition than I could have coped with at the time, so it was head down and mouth shut. After all, I had incontrovertible evidence of the truth of all this from the New Testament, which, of course, was the 'inerrant word of God'. Any doubt was my problem.

Locked into my intellectual paradigms though I was, something of whatever it is we refer to when we speak of 'spirit' broke through from time to time. One day my wife and I arrived home from a day out with the children. They went straight out to play and we two went into our dining room with cups of tea. Immediately a sense of profound peace descended on me. It was a deeper feeling than the one I usually got from having no children about. The experience was not ecstatic but gentle, a 'peace that passes all understanding' as Paul put it. My wife didn't experience it at all, but patiently sat with me as I whispered, 'Can't you feel it?' I could not comprehend how she could not feel the gathered silence; it was so tangible. I don't know how long we sat there because for me, once again, time had stood still. I can imagine my wife getting really frustrated and wanting to get more tea, but she didn't. Even if she had, I don't think her activity could have broken the magic of that moment.

Pennies from Heaven

We began to attend a Charismatic house church more frequently, though the Gospel Hall was still our main base. But eventually we realised we needed to commit ourselves one way or the other, and left the Gospel Hall to give ourselves fully to the house church. As soon as an opportunity arrived, we cut ourselves adrift from our Brethren base and went to live in the midst of the house church community, the circumstances of which I considered to be the direct interventions of "God".

Friends in our new church had also decided to move house and gave us first refusal on their property. We were ten percent short on the price they wanted, but they generously accepted the offer we could make and we moved in. Then, one member of the house church decided we needed to be mobile and gave us his car. We were riding the crest of a religious wave. I thought such events were like the miracles of provision spoken of by our evangelist friend Ray, in Malta. "God" was with us, of that there could be no doubt.

I started to become loosely involved with the wider Charismatic leadership in Bristol and visited other leadership teams in different parts of the country. It was a heady time and our days were filled with a lot of hugging and hallelu-ing. "God" was on the move, it seemed, and many people were being drawn into the movement, mainly from traditional church backgrounds. Some moved out of their churches into house-churches, as we had done; some traditional churches became centres of Charismatic Christianity themselves. St. Philip and St. James's church (known as Pip and Jay's), in the centre of Bristol, was packed out every Sunday with a happy-clappy crowd. People spoke in tongues, the whole congregation sang in tongues, people prophesied, the sick and sad were prayed over, hymns were sung rapturously with much waving of arms and people danced in the aisles. We all left as high as kites and without a pill between us. I understand it is much the same to this day.

My wife didn't get as deeply involved in Charismatic Christianity as I did but she didn't prevent me from throwing myself into it wholeheartedly —a tendency in me often criticised. The children, all under twelve at this time, tagged along. I think they enjoyed their Charismatic Sunday School more than the one they'd attended at the conservative Brethren Church. My life with the children was generally very happy then. We had a lot of fun together, even though there was never quite enough money. The house-church movement did a lot to promote good family life and we received useful teaching from visiting speakers, which helped us hone our parenting skills. However, my wife and I were slowly realising storm clouds were piling up on the horizon of our relationship. The atmosphere between us got progressively worse.

The Fire Damped

The beginning of the end of faith for me was when I'd applied for a job which involved my taking some aptitude tests. These revealed I was actually considerably brighter than either my education or career to date had shown me to be. Quite unexpectedly I got the job as a programmed-learning author. For the first time in my life it was a joy to wake up on Monday mornings and realise I could go to work again. However, every silver lining has a cloud, as they say. With hindsight I suspect the man who recruited me probably thought of me as his male equivalent to Elisa Doolittle. Here was I, without a qualification to my name, working with a team of young university graduates! Initially I was a star. I performed better than most of my colleagues but that was only until my mentor discovered I was religious. It came about like this: The company was part of the Imperial Tobacco group, and so each month every employee received a free gift of fifty cigarettes. When my issue arrived I refused it on principle.

'But you must have friends who smoke,' they said. 'You could give them away.'

I told them I was a Christian and refused to have anything to do with cigarettes. I felt very righteous and pleased at the confusion I had sown. They really didn't know what to do in this situation and were rather embarrassed by my stand. I guess someone else got my ration because the matter was never raised again, but from then on my relationship with my manager began to deteriorate. It became clear that he hated religious people with a passion and, from having been unable to do anything wrong, I could now do nothing right. Over the next few months the situation got progressively worse. I would take him a piece of work and he would point out all the errors. I'd sort out the errors he'd identified and present it again. This time he'd find different errors, though they weren't errors, just different ways of expressing the same thing. I was at my wits end. There was no way of pleasing the man. I was taken off meaningful projects and given odd editing jobs to do. From having woken each day looking forward to going to work, I now felt sick in my stomach at the thought of what I may have to face.

Although working life had become so difficult, the intelligent and well informed conversations I was having with my colleagues had begun to broaden my mind. I discovered intellectual fulfilment outside my religion and gradually found my need for heavy Bible study subsided. It was at this time the storm clouds that had long been gathering over our marriage began to shed rain. Through my work, I had 'moved on' and become fulfilled. Suddenly I was no longer the failed student, mechanic, musician and soldier. Despite the difficulties at work I was a modestly successful writer who had begun to explore a wider intellectual landscape. I wanted to share all my new-found treasures with my wife but this was never going to be possible, and so we entered a period of severe frustration. I was no longer the person my wife had married; she was no longer the kind of person I wanted to be in a relationship with. We never argued much but rubbed along. Our four children gave us enough to occupy ourselves, leaving little time to think much about our troubled relationship. One of the outcomes of this was that it became much more difficult for me to manage the family adequately. Our eldest daughter was now in her teens and, whereas we had known what we were doing as parents up until then, our immaturity meant parenting teenagers became a big challenge. I deeply regret I could not be conscious of many of the family's real needs at the time. My life so far had enabled me to ignore my real feelings. As a result I could feel passably OK even when I wasn't—I guess this is 'normal' for most people. I dealt with problems in my marriage in the same way.

At about this time I was introduced to Lyall Watson's book *Supernature*. What a revelation that was! I discovered, rather than many 'miraculous' phenomena being supernatural, it was possible to find a rational explanation for them. I liked Watson's apparently open-minded approach. If he didn't know, or couldn't prove his ideas, then he said so, leaving mystery securely in place but opening the way to future understanding. It was my first encounter with someone who was not a Christian but who exhibited the qualities of what I was beginning to recognise as 'spirituality'. His writing was a complete contrast to that of the religious authors I'd been used to reading. Christian authors were all absolutely certain they were right and wouldn't bend to any interpretation of 'Truth' that didn't come with a verse from the Bible attached to it. Watson spoke of amazing phenomena without needing to establish a cause, thus leaving me wondering at mystery—something fundamentalism rarely lets you do.

In 1974 I was made 'redundant', a euphemism for 'the manager can't stand your Christianity any more'. A sympathetic senior manager told me he'd made a mistake with the paper work so the company would have to pay me two month's severance pay instead of one. So I didn't rush off to find a job but dug the garden for a few weeks. Between digging and spreading muck I pondered on what to do.

I went to the Executive Counselling Service for some guidance, which led to my applying for a course at college. Even though I didn't have a first degree, I was accepted on a post-graduate course to train as a careers counsellor. My experience to date was accepted as evidence of my ability to do the course and I found myself among twenty-eight lively young graduates. I was elated to discover that, in this academic context, I could, not only hold my own, but do better than most. In studying psychology I found out about inverse correlations, and quickly realised I had one of my own: the difference between my sense of fulfilment intellectually and my dwindling sense of fulfilment in things religious. My faith was not on as secure a foundation as I'd thought it was. Sadly neither was my marriage.

Reflections and Revelations

As I devoured books on psychology and sociology, I discovered many of those things which I had regarded as 'spiritual' were in fact the result of common psychological or sociological phenomena. For instance, the energy that raised the emotional temperature of a meeting was not necessarily spiritual, but psychological. The inspirational speakers I'd held in adulation, were just that—inspirational speakers. They knew, either through instinct or training, how to evoke a response in the minds of their audience.

Theories of group dynamics showed me how people in groups could easily be caught up in a social 'rush' and be led to believe things, and do things, they might not do in other circumstances. For instance, I learned about Solomon Asch, who conducted a famous experiment in 1951, which demonstrated how easy it was to get people to conform to ideas through the pressure of opinion around them.[4] He drew three lines on a piece of paper and put it on a notice board. Groups of people were asked to decide, without measuring them, which line was the longest. In fact all the lines were of the same length. When he 'seeded' a group with a strong personality who insisted that this or that line was the longest, the majority of the group would tend to agree. It began to dawn on me how foolish I'd been; how easily I'd been caught up in other people's certainties and on how flimsy a basis was my faith.

My new understanding of psychology also helped me to see what was going on when I was facing confrontations over faith. I had certainly projected my own fears on those who threatened my beliefs. One such projection became apparent during the Festival of Light anti-pornography campaigns. Having not really come to terms with my own sexual

---

4 Asch, S. E.. Studies of independence and conformity: A minority of one against a unanimous majority (1956). Psychological Monograph

frustrations, I found my mind contorted with hatred towards those who published or sold such blatantly evil material. At the same time, I longed to take a closer look! There was nothing in my belief system that could alleviate my agony and no one I could trust enough to share my problem with. All I could do was to keep beating myself up mentally over my deep feeling of guilt. I had developed digestive problems and the nervous rash of my teen years had returned. Such psychosomatic illnesses were clearly symptoms of my continuing inner turmoil.

Within a few months of joining the college course I began to find a new personal identity. My old, religious, identity didn't fit any more. I was becoming a new person and probably nearer to my authentic self, but I wasn't there yet. As I became more confident, my physical symptoms vanished. Even so I can now see my new personal identity was still largely ego-centric.

At this time I was beginning to finally acknowledge that my marriage of fifteen years was not a good fit. My wife was finding it increasingly difficult to relate to the person I'd become and I to accept her as she was. There was a lot of tension in the house, yet there was sufficient loyalty and religion, as well as a lot of children, to keep us together for a few more years.

Once a person begins to emerge from a false sense of self, all relationships begin to change and I began to develop doubts about my relationship with members of the church. I had for some time been concerned that some people opened up readily about their personal problems in House Church meetings, but many didn't. Although I knew some of them were facing difficult issues in their lives, they didn't seem able to share them with others to get support. Instead of leaving things to "God", I decided to set an example but, as usual, probably got carried away by my enthusiasm.

Too Much Heart, Not Enough Sleeve.

One evening I opened up with the group about some of the problems I was experiencing. My intention had been to show leadership by demonstrating that it was OK to have weaknesses and needs. However, that wasn't the way people saw it, especially not my fellow leaders. They seemed to think the weaknesses I had shared with them were an impediment to my rôle and I was abruptly dropped from the small leadership group. They were quite right in what they did, for I wasn't as adequate internally as I may have appeared outwardly. A short time after this, another member of the wider group fell seriously from grace, admitting to having done far worse things than I had. The response of the leadership to him seemed to me to be far more supportive than I had experienced. Maybe I felt a bit jealous. I certainly felt hurt that I had not been supported and nurtured in the same way. I can now recognise this as the response of the ego's 'false self', but then, I just felt angry.

Chapter Five

The Fire Extinguished

The 'wave', on whose crest my faith had been riding a few short years before, began to curl as it ran headlong for solid ground. It finally crashed upon the beach when, as a result of my success on the careers guidance course, I was head-hunted for a job in Gloucestershire. However, the church leaders got together and, having prayed about it, though without me, advised that I should not accept the job. It was the beginning of a 'discipleship' movement, which advocated submission to leaders. It now seems strange anyone should feel "God" would guide them directly about someone else's life without the person being party to it, but this was what we were asked to believe at the time. (The movement eventually saw the folly of this idea). I suppose some people were glad to have others make decisions for them, as I had been when I was a child, but I was beginning to mature—albeit rather late in life. In many ways I had been a spiritual infant who needed to be kept on the walking reins and regularly cleaned up, but I realise now many of those who reputedly had charge of my soul were in the same condition. Without recognising how the ego's 'false self' operates, it is impossible to avoid its negative influence on one's life, however religious one may be. This applies to every aspect of living, whether religious or secular. I had grown sceptical about some of the beliefs I once held sacred and this scepticism melted the glue that bound me, not only to the beliefs, but to those who held the beliefs. When your relationship with "God" is utterly dependent upon your beliefs, it is necessary to ask whether your relationship is actually with "God" or with what you believe.

Moving On

My new job came at a time when three of the children had reached a critical point in their education and relocating the family would have been too disruptive. So for the next couple of years I travelled daily up to Gloucestershire. We continued to attend the house church, but I stopped preaching on the Methodist circuit and found it difficult to be as wholehearted about religion as I had been. Gradually my attendance at meetings became more and more sporadic. I then found that many of those whom I had counted as my friends in the church deserted me. Sadly, it seemed they could only relate to me through their religion and I've only maintained contact with one couple from those days. Here's how I summed up this period some years after the event:

Those were high days.
At any minute
we were about to change the world.
We blended words with passion,
intoxicated with the sounds
that babbled forth,
verbose as a brook in spate
and twice as noisy.

The words wound around
each phrase,
endowing it with bits of truth,
binding the words
to us and us to each other.
These same few words,
melodic scales,
built symphonies of sound
that filled our universe
so full, it drowned
all other music but our own.

These were my constellations,
fixed, immutable, secure,
lighting my path,
but darkening my mind

in all but one corner of the roof top,
where I was locked in
with the brawling woman
of my own thoughts.

And then the words evaporated
like dew in summer.
There came a kind of peace
(or rather lack of war)
a truce,
which left me
shell-shocked and still.

For ten long years
my soul languished
while my body did
what bodies want to do.
Then an inkling
followed by another,
helped me to know for sure
that I knew nothing.

And now truth
reveals herself at morning,
(sometimes in frost,
sometimes in gentle dew).

Unexpected,
sometimes uninvited,
she comes in the afternoon,
the evening
and the night.

And when she comes,
the child within me leaps for joy,
recognising her in all her many guises.

And those who shared
their substances with me
still share their substances
with one another,
but I seek those
who share, not substances,
but Self.

In those 'ten long years' when my soul was languishing, I was enjoying a happy and successful career. I quickly got promotion and my work was so fulfilling that once again, every morning I woke up looking forward to going to work. This success helped to relieve some of the problems in our marriage. It wasn't that we argued a lot; indeed, one of the problems was that we hardly argued at all. Neither did we discuss much, certainly not about things which I considered important. We had very different interests and there just didn't seem to be anything we could share. The awkward silences of our phone calls sixteen years before, were little to do with our immaturity but symptomatic of something much deeper. Not being the kind of person that can leave a problem alone, I began to take steps to make my wife into the kind of person I thought I wanted to be with. I'm very pleased I never succeeded. She's fine as she is.

From Religion to Spirituality

Three minor yet significant events changed the direction of my life. The first was a television series, broadcast on the UK's Channel Four, called "The Power of Myth". In it Bill Moyers, an American journalist, conducted a series of interviews with the world's leading comparative mythologist, Joseph Campbell. Campbell explained how the great mythological stories of the past weren't simply the efforts of ignorant and fearful people to describe the world they lived in but were, more importantly, metaphors that arose out of the unconscious which informed them how to live. My careers-counselling training had given me a sufficient smattering of psychology to appreciate this concept and I began to see my religious experience in a completely new light. As I started to understand the operation of symbols in the myths, I began to understand what my heart had actually been responding to in the scriptures. It occurred to me that maybe my religious experience hadn't been entirely wasted after all. Perhaps, albeit by accident, what I'd experienced was spiritual, though not supernatural as I'd imagined. At the time I couldn't fully appreciate the reality of what was going on because my religious doctrines had got in the way. As Joseph Conrad said, '*Words, as is well known, are the great foes of reality.*'

Broadening Vision

At this point I still wasn't yet ready to take my spirituality neat but now my mixers tended to be intellectual rather than religious. On reflection, it was a process I probably needed to go through to bring me to a place where I could know what was safe to let go and what to keep. I bought a transcript of "The Power of Myth" programme as soon as it was published, and it led me on a new and exciting journey. I bought copies of the "Bhagavad Gita" and the "Upanishads" by Juan Mascaro and found the forewords alone tantalisingly instructive. Soon these books took the place of my Bible. But I didn't ditch the Bible; indeed, my copy of Mascaro's "Bhagavad Gita" is covered with pencilled cross-references to the New Testament. No doubt this is due partly to the fact that Mascaro's translation has obviously been influenced by his own Christian background.

What arose out of Indian mysticism led to my next major paradigm shift. I began to understand that, whatever it was I'd formerly referred to as 'God', was both transcendent and immanent. In the past, those concepts were confused in my mind. When I prayed, it was to a god who was immanent, a father in whose presence I imagined I sat. Yet he always seemed transcendent, in Heaven, unknowable, unfathomable and remote. After all, most of the time he didn't answer my prayers, or at least not in the way I expected and he didn't intervene when, really, I thought he should have done. I found I had to rethink "God", for whatever he, she or it was in reality, could not possibly fit my narrow fundamentalist Christian view. Now I began to understand that whatever it was I referred to as 'God' was beyond personality and was not 'out there' trying to do things in here but right here in me, doing things through me out there.

A great change began to take place in me. As Ken Wilber says, *'We begin elitist, but if we stay on the journey, we always become egalitarian. Always!'* Certainly, few people could have been more elitist than me but as my spiritual horizons began to expand, I realised spirituality was far more wonderful and widespread than I had ever imagined. Most importantly, I learned that Christians weren't the only ones to experience it.

We eventually moved to a new home in Stroud at a point when all the children had grown into teenagers with all the usual accompanying angst. Work life was wonderful. Home life became increasingly difficult. I brooded on the differences between my wife and myself—never a good thing to do—and the differences grew into monsters. All my efforts to change my wife into the person I thought she should be had failed. By 1982 the three oldest children were either at college or working away from home, and I decided we should have a trial separation. I found myself a room in a big house in the next village and hoped to find a new life. As is usual in such circumstances, I only found a new room in which to live my old life, except it wasn't altogether my old life. I had jumped off the boat without a life jacket and was adrift in a hostile ocean.

My wife courageously supported me in this venture but within a very short time I could see she was becoming ill. Part of me was crying out for freedom, yet there were strong promptings from within me and I knew with certainty what I had to do. I moved back into the family home. It was the only way the promptings would give me peace. I knew I had to learn to accept my wife just as she was, and I did so. We stayed together for another twelve years, though we lived largely separate lives. Although our separation only lasted for three months I regret that I totally misjudged the effect it would have on my youngest daughter. She felt she'd lost a trusted friend, which deeply affected her adolescence and left scars which remained with her for many years. I'm pleased to say that they have healed and we have put all this behind us.

In 1989 my mother died. She had suffered with a heart problem since she was eight years old, though she rarely let it stop her from leading an active life. She had remained a Congregationalist, attending the United Reformed Church when the Congregationalists joined forces with English Presbyterians and others in 1972. Dad was devastated at losing his best friend after fifty-one years of marriage. He had attended the URC with Mum but, after she died, found the local church wasn't very supportive of him and so ceased going. Nobody contacted him, so he went back to some of his Eastern thinking and read books on Buddhism and Hinduism, which meant we had some interesting conversations. He also continued to think a lot about philosophy and is the only motor mechanic I have known to have read *Plato's Republic*. I'm grateful to all I've inherited from him.

Letting Go

In the early nineties, came my next significant paradigm shift. I read a book called "What the Buddha Never Taught" by Tim Ward*. It's about his year in a Buddhist Wat in Thailand and I came away from reading it with the clear feeling that I knew nothing. This was not a negative impression. On the contrary, it was for me a 'Damascus road' experience. The inspirational passage that catalysed this truth in my mind was: 'We've all created an illusion, a thing we want to believe in so much we let it torment us all life long.' For the first time in my life I became fully conscious that everything I thought I knew was, in reality, an illusion. Two and a half millennia after Socrates it clicked that, like him, all I could really know

* When I started writing this book I couldn't find or even remember the title of the book or the name of its author. Then a wonderful synchronicity occurred. Over lunch, I was telling friends my experience and was asked, "His name wasn't Tim Ward, was it?" I said that I believed it might have been. Tim was the son of good friends they had made, when John had worked in Canada. He had given Shirley and John a signed copy of his book, *What the Buddha Never Taught,* and she lent me her copy.

was that I can't know. As I learned more about the human brain, I came to see that all thought is an illusion; what's in my mind is only an impression of the reality that's out there. When I see, I only see what my brain makes of frequencies of light which come through the retina of my eye. When I hear, I only hear what my brain makes of the frequencies of sound which come into my ear. It's so obvious, yet I had never thought of it that way before.

It helped me realise that if I don't truly understand the truth about the things I think of as solid and coloured entities, how could I truly understand frail ideas wrapped up in words like religious beliefs?

As a charismatic Christian I'd wanted passionately to believe in my beliefs, yet I suffered great emotional torment as a result. Suddenly, I was overjoyed to discover it was actually OK to know nothing — I could safely let go of it all. Before I could be full, I had to be empty. Before I could experience 'being', I had to stop 'becoming'. This was surely a principle which Jesus spoke of in Matthew Chapter Five when he said 'Blessed are the poor in spirit', a principle he epitomised. The word 'poor' here, I discovered, means 'beggarly' - not a down-and-out, but one who realises he or she has nothing. I found the Tao Teh Ching speaks in several places of a similar principle. In passage 37 we read, *'Learning consists of daily accumulating; the practice of the Tao consists in daily diminishing.'* The Bhagavad Gita is a whole treatise on not being attached to desire or fear. In chapter three Krishna says, '*By sacrifice thou shalt multiply and obtain all thy desires.*'

I would have to visit this idea again and again over the years. I used to boast of this illumination, saying I'd now reached the point when I could write what I actually knew in large letters on the back of a postage stamp. But I came to realise that was far too great a boast. I was right in the first place. When it comes to the divine I can know absolutely *nothing*. We humans are constantly tempted to think words are important in helping us to experience the divine—a trillion books attest to this particular illusion. It's essential to constantly remind ourselves words can obstruct truth far more easily than reveal it. Maybe the best we can hope for is that the words reveal to us something about ourselves that has to be dealt with, so that we can get beyond the words into the true experience; but more of that later.

For some people emptying themselves of previous concepts may be easy. For me, a subliminal nagging persisted, by ideas and feelings that had pervaded the deepest recesses of the psyche. It took a long time before I was able to wash away the remains of most of the old concepts and begin to embrace uncertainty wholeheartedly. During this time my wife would tell me, quite rightly, I was simply making things too complicated. She has remained true to her Christian beliefs throughout and there is no reason why she should not. But for me, it seemed change was inevitable

In "Thus Spake Zarathustra", Nietzsche speaks of holding only '*a hands-breadth of firm land*', in other words of certainty.[5] To achieve a' '*hand's breadth'* of firm intellectual ground may be all we can reasonably aspire to—probably far more than we should expect. To have <u>all</u> the answers, as I'd thought I'd had, is to hold a sizeable acreage and this now seems to me to be the height of absurdity.

That life holds only uncertainty, far from being nihilist or defeatist, is the only certainty we have. T.S. Eliot expressed this paradox perfectly:

'In order to arrive at what you do not know
You must go by a way which is the way of ignorance.
In order to possess what you do not possess
You must go by the way of dispossession.
In order to arrive at what you are
You must go through the way in which you are not.
And what you do not know is the only thing you know
And what you own is what you do not own
And where you are is where you are not. [6]

5 Friedrich Nietzsche, Thus Spake Zarathustra, Trans R.J Hollingdale, Penguin books
6 *East Coker*, T.S. Eliot, from Four Quartets, T.S. Eliot

Finding the True Self

Who I had thought I was had arisen out of what I thought I knew. But what I knew was only someone else's words. I was largely the creation of my own mind-stuff, or worse, other people's mind stuff. The real me existed but it was buried under a mountain of knowledge. As Meister Eckhart, the 13th Century German mystic said,

> *'A human being has so many skins inside, covering the depths of the heart. We know so many things, but we don't know ourselves! Why, thirty or forty skins or hides, as thick and hard as an ox's or a bear's, cover the soul. Go into your own ground and learn to know yourself there.'*

I thought my 'True Self' was the person I had constructed from the mind-stuff I'd accrued from my life experiences, including—perhaps especially including—the religious ones, but this construction is really 'the person I'm not', my ego's 'false self'. I began to realise that to be truly 'born again' would necessitate my learning to recognise my 'false self', not saying a prescribed prayer and ticking the boxes on a doctrinal check list. Once I shone the light of consciousness on my 'false self' it would begin the process of transformation.

I began to see the death and resurrection of Jesus in a completely different way. The death and resurrection wasn't so much about being a sacrifice to appease an angry "God", though this had been the orthodox understanding for the best part of two millennia. For me, it is about the experience of awakening to the 'True Self'. When that happens, the 'false self' is inevitably transformed (dies and is resurrected, so to speak). It's inevitable because the true and the false, like light and darkness, cannot exist together. But I will expand on this later.

To get to this point of realisation required a considerable amount of intellectual demolition on my part, which is a messy job at best. There is a danger when you raise a new building on the old ground that it will be just as solid and impregnable as the original. Therefore I hope what I'm doing, rather than erecting a building, is planting a garden. Unlike a building, a garden changes with the seasons. You can root out old plants and put in new ones. Although the garden changes season to season, year to year, it is still recognisable as a garden—a place in which to sit and meditate and listen. As Rumi wrote, '*Personalities are born once. A mystic, many times.*'

Mind Changer

Such thinking as this developed as I cycled the quiet roads and lanes of the Cotswold Hills on Sundays, while my wife went to church. Then the local authority for which I worked offered me a very good redundancy/early retirement package and I set up as a freelance journalist. My spare time journalism had paid for three daughters' weddings and a trip to America over the previous seven years and I realised I could probably find enough work to satisfy our smaller household. And so I did.

Then people began to ask me to run training courses in business computing, which I had been writing about, and a course in business English materialised, so I began to build a training consultancy. At the same time I was heavily involved with a poetry workshop and a writers' group. These fed both my intellectual and spiritual needs, and brought me into contact with a lot of interesting people, including Elizabeth.

Elizabeth became a good friend, someone I could talk to about things that interested us both. A graduate in English, with a sharp mind, she was able to discuss books, writers, poetry and history, though I never shared my ideas about spirituality with her. On one of our visits to her house, my wife told Elizabeth she was glad I had her as a friend, because I could talk about things with her that my wife had no interest in. I had other ladies among my friends and it was all very platonic. However, after eighteen months or so, Elizabeth and I began to realise something very special was developing between us, though we never spoke our minds to each other at the time.

My wife and I continued to live increasingly separate lives until we reached the breaking point. I won't go into the details, some of which I regret, but we eventually agreed to part once and for all. During the lead up to our final separation, which I had for some long time become frighteningly aware was impending, I felt as if I was being split down the middle. My relationship with my wife had never been bad, for me it had simply been empty. Yet my heart was telling me that if we stayed together we'd simply dwindle into a fruitless old age. I'd watched elderly couples in bars staring emptily into space without having anything to say to each other any more. That was already beginning to happen to us. I'd even begun to ensure that if we dined out, we did so with friends, just to keep the conversation going. But the thought of the hurt that would be inevitable reduced me to tears night after night.

Telling my wife our marriage was over was the most difficult thing I have ever had to do in my life and the pain of that separation, even though I knew it to be the right thing to do, stayed with me for two years. During that time I spent many hours out on my bike grieving, but I gradually realised what I was grieving over was not so much the person, but the relationship—that third mysterious entity which comes into existence when two people become deeply involved with each other. Even though I suffered a sense of loss almost daily throughout this period, and wept a good deal, at the same time I experienced a strange sense of peace. Whatever the theology I had once held about marriage being unbreakable, I knew the relationship had had to be dissolved—for both our sakes.

I think my wife knew this too for she never asked to be reconciled. When our daughter Jinny gave birth to her second child, Elizabeth went to my wife's house hoping to surreptitiously leave some flowers on the doorstep. Unexpectedly my wife opened the door, accepted the flowers and kissed Elizabeth on the cheek. She is truly a remarkable lady.

My main concern was for the family. The girls had taken the situation fairly well but my son was so upset he wouldn't speak to me at all. That really hurt and it took a year or so to begin to heal the rift. But heal it did and the family rallied to cope with the new situation.

The children all eventually accepted the break-up had been a good thing, and that Elizabeth and I are as good together as we think we are. If

I had remained a fundamentalist Christian, my marriage to my wife would have probably stayed intact and we would have been one of those old couples sitting in the pub without anything to talk about, not even religion. I now have no doubt that, without that break, the next part of my spiritual journey would not have been possible. Whoever "God" is, He, She or It is no respecter of doctrine.

A Dreamer and a Quaker

I continued to read and re-read spiritual books and spent many hours contemplating spiritual issues while cycling the hills and valleys around our Cotswold home. Liz and I had begun to attend the Anglican church in the village, Elizabeth having been confirmed into that faith. As soon as it was practical we had our marriage blessed by the vicar in a beautiful ceremony with a church packed full of family and friends. However, there was little in the church services that resonated with me and I found it impossible to recite the creed or identify with the hymns, so gradually my church attendance became more sporadic.

I never felt the need to seek any other spiritual outlet, nor did I meet anyone with whom I could converse about spiritual matters. Then in 2003 we moved to rural Herefordshire, one of the most sparsely populated areas of England, and here I began a new phase in my spiritual development.

In 2006, having ploughed a lone spiritual furrow for some thirty years, I had a dream. I was on a high stepladder outside a redundant church building, taking corrugated iron sheets away from a large stained glass window. I was very conscious of people walking on the pavement below and the need to ensure I didn't drop any tools on them. I was significantly aware I was preparing the building as a home. When I awoke, I pondered this and felt maybe I should find a spiritual home for myself, but I couldn't imagine finding one in any of the local churches. Who would have a heretic like me? Then a friend, a retired Anglican clergyman, with whom I had some of my most edifying spiritual conversations, said that he occasionally attended a Quaker meeting and thought I might find it interesting. So on an April Sunday morning I drove over to the nearby village of Almeley and spent an hour or so with Quakers in the 17th Century meeting house. The warmth of welcome, I was relieved to discover, was not driven by desperation for new members. What influenced me most was the profound experience of 'presence' in the largely silent meeting. I decided I would return and have been doing so regularly ever since. In 2008, to Elizabeth's amusement and bemusement, I committed myself to membership of the Religious Society of Friends—I became a Quaker[7]. To get to this point required a considerable amount of deconstruction, and that is the subject of the rest of this book.

7 In 2020 I felt called to leave Quakers, having served as an elder for nearly three years. My 12 years sojourn with The Religious Society of Friends had taught me much but I had reached a point where I needed to move out of organised religion altogether to further spiritual work which was opening to me, work which meant that identifying with any one religious group could be an impediment.

PART II

From fundamentalism to faith

'For last year's words belong to last year's language
And next year's words await another voice.'
T.S. Eliot, Little Gidding.

As Richard Rohr says, 'Without some deconstruction everything becomes idolatrous', so I want to make it clear that, in deconstructing my old beliefs, I do not seek, as the New Atheists do, to destroy religion. Rather I seek to go beyond it, to transcend it, for that is what I believe all religious people are called to do. Neither do I recommend that the path I am taking should be emulated, and must add a 'health warning'. The danger of deconstructing is that we start constructing a new ideology on the old foundations. This is especially a problem for those whose relationship with what they think of as "God" is dependent on what they think they should believe about "God". Such a relationship is not with 'The Divine' but with belief itself. It's 'falling in love with love' as the old song puts it. The path of deconstruction is likely to be one of ultimate simplifying to the point of unknowing. Here's Richard Rohr again:

> *'When you put knowing together with not knowing, and even become willing not to know, you have this marvellous phenomenon called faith, which allows you to keep an open horizon, an open field. You can thus remain in a humble and wondrous beginner's mind, even as you grow older, maybe even more so.'*[8]

Religious doctrines arise from ideas and points of view laid down one upon the other over the centuries. Rather than revealing 'truth', as every religion claims, doctrine often diffuses truth so we only 'see through a glass darkly', as Paul put it. However, despite its obvious disadvantages, religion has helped countless millions of people to find their way through the complexities of human existence to peace. I found it important to

8 Rohr, Richard. Silent Compassion: Finding God in Contemplation (p. 12). Franciscan Media.

understand how religion arose, in particular Christianity, what its purpose has been and what is its true relationship to reality.

When I was a boy the story of Theseus and the Minotaur fascinated me. The young prince was helped in his heroic adventure by Ariadne, the daughter of his enemy. She provided him with a thread to follow, so that having gone into the maze and killed the Minotaur, he could find his way out again. Religion is like a maze. The way out is the way in. Having been constructed by reason, religion can be deconstructed by reason and so this section is my Ariadne's thread.

In sharing my thoughts with you I realise speculation and opinion have never brought anybody into an experience of the divine. The best we can hope for is that they may peel back those 'many skins' that 'cover the depths of the heart', that Eckhart spoke of. We may then become more open, more receptive and more vulnerable to whatever experience grace bestows.

Chapter Six

Where's the Inerrancy?

The most *fundamental* fundamental of fundamentalism is that the Bible is the inerrant word of "God". Without this tenet fundamentalism crumbles into the dust, for its very existence has to be based on absolute certainty. Take away this belief, I'd thought as a Christian, and you could believe anything you liked. There just had to be some immutable foundations upon which to build the house. Otherwise, like the house built on the sand of which Jesus spoke, it would be destroyed by the wind and flood of human argument. It never occurred to me to question just how immutable my foundations were. That would have been a much too threatening thing to do.

The Inerrancy Battle

In my fundamentalist days any doubts I'd had about the inerrancy of the word of "God", I'd ignored. Psychologists call this 'cognitive dissonance', which is the discomfort of holding two or more conflicting ideas at the same time. To handle this we tend to compartmentalise our thoughts and we're pretty good at that. And with thoughts which were sometimes as irrational as mine it was essential to compartmentalise, if I wanted to stay true to the faith, that is. So I rationalised any evidence about the Bible contrary to the beliefs I shared with my fellow church members—even those which ran counter to the laws of physics. I reasoned that with "God", nothing was impossible. So obsessed with this idea was I that one day I ritually crossed out the word 'impossible' from my Oxford Dictionary.

One perennial problem that challenged my beliefs was the regular occurrences of genocide commanded by "God" in the Old Testament. How could the loving "God" that Jesus spoke of order my Biblical heroes to slaughter innocent women and children? In Deuteronomy 2:32, for instance, the Israelites are commanded to wipe out all the men, women and children of Heshbon, but to keep all the livestock and plunder for themselves. Such action was surely no better than that of the pagan Vikings who raided Britain in the Dark Ages. To compound the problem, I found another story of genocide in the first book of Samuel. Here, "God" commands King Saul to destroy every man, woman and child of the Amalekites and all their possessions. Again, this seemed to me totally contrary to what I understood God's loving and merciful nature to be. The act became doubly obnoxious when "God" made Saul forfeit his crown for keeping the livestock. When I raised it with elders of the church they merely said that people lived according to the light they had at the time, which is undoubtedly true. But I couldn't understand why the 'inspired' word of "God" condoned such behaviour.

But in those days my ability to accept that which I didn't understand came naturally. There were many aspects of my life in the Army which I either didn't understand or disagreed with but, like everyone else, I just got on with it. We often quoted Lord Alfred Tennyson: '*Ours not to reason why, ours but to do and die.*' Obedience was what was required by the Army and my 'faith' demanded the same.

Meaning and Myth

Sadly, we westerners have downgraded the word 'myth' to mean something that is untrue—the 'urban myth' for instance. My new understanding began with my thinking that a myth is a story which *contains* truth. Then the realisation hit me that it is impossible for words to contain anything at all. If I don't know the meaning of a word, it contains nothing as far as I'm concerned. I came to see that words and other symbols, rather than being conveyors of meaning, are catalysts of meaning. Rumi expresses this as language 'alchemising into amber'.[9] One of the most precious crumbs of truth I've come to understand is that meaning is not in the words, but in me.

Even so, thoughts communicated in words do not always communicate at the level of consciousness. Usually, when I hear words, their reference comes alive in my mind and the meaning they symbolise is provoked into consciousness. Studies have shown that the sound of a person's name

9 Soul Houses, Rumi—*Bridge to the Soul*, Coleman Barks, Harper Collins.

evokes a physiological response in that person even when the mention of the name is not directed at him or her. On the other hand, words sometimes fall on stony ground—mention a name which I don't recognise and it has no effect on me whatsoever. All symbols, whether images or words, operate by calling meaning into consciousness.

I also came to understand that there seem to be two modes in which understanding arises in the mind. These are handled by the two separate, though interconnected, hemispheres of the cerebral cortex: left and right. Rational thought seems to be dealt with mainly by the left brain in which linear logic and reason takes place. These are the kind of processes which enable me to know about things, people, events and the like. They rely heavily on what is already known and tend to extrapolate ideas about new encounters from that. This is the source of our paradigms, which was fine when all we had to think about was survival, but our minds and our culture have moved a long way since then. We now have to deal with abstract constructs: things that don't exist in the real world and such conditions as multiculturalism, which brings us into contact with people whose customs are foreign to our way of thinking.

The right brain, on the other hand, tends to think more holistically. It is concerned more with the here and now, in what is human, rather than mechanical. Psychiatrist Iain McGilchrist quotes Decety & Chaminade:,

> *'Self-awareness, empathy, identification with others, and more generally inter-subjective processes, are largely dependent upon . . . right hemisphere resources.'*[10]

Right brain knowledge tends to be experiential. It is knowledge that has become embodied and therefore seems to have more to do with the right brain's connection with the more primitive part of the brain which deals with movement and feeling. There are many things I only know at this level—how to walk, for instance. Nobody explained to me the principles of walking. I gained the knowledge by doing it. Describing

10 Decety & Chaminade, 2003, p. 591, quoted in McGilchrist, Iain. The Master and His Emissary

how a human being walks is almost impossible. Try it. In the process you'll get an insight into what complex processes your right brain accomplishes with little or no help from your left brain.

Of course understanding can be both right and left brain orientated. The words my left brain processed when I was told my mother had died may have been in rational mode, but the meaning they provoked in me was far from rational. Left-brain processing may be thought of as logical thought and right-brain processing as poetic or symbolic thought, though this is a gross generalisation. The difference is that with rational thought I have to make the meaning fit the words (I have to rationalise); with poetic or symbolic thought I have to allow the words to find meaning in me.

If this is so that I am led to consider that if meaning is in me, the actual words cannot of themselves contain meaning or truth — not even in the Bible. In which case, neither can they be inerrant. Perhaps this helps to explain why there are so many interpretations of scripture—even among fundamentalists. Once we begin to rationalise that which should be experienced, we deny ourselves the active experience and settle for passive understanding.

Words and symbols can provoke meaning within us but our predilections, preferences and prejudices colour the meaning we find. I once mentioned the name of a liberal theologian to a Methodist minister friend and he responded that he disagreed with practically everything the man had ever said. Yet someone else, who had attended a talk by the same liberal theologian, said that for the first time in her life she understood what kind of Christian she was. This is the nature of words: they provoke different meanings, and indeed feelings, in different people, especially if they conflict with what a person already thinks. That's why it's essential to understand that words are only symbols. They never ever represent themselves but always point to something beyond their shape and sound.

Myths, then, are simply visual symbols painted in words. Because my fundamentalist friends and I had not understood the pre-modern mythological mind, we'd got ourselves into a convoluted theological mess.

We had been reading symbols as facts and, as Campbell says, that's like reading 'steak' on the menu then eating the menu!

The light shed (or drawn into consciousness) by Campbell's book, “The Power of Myth”, led me to a new way of reading the Bible and anything else 'spiritual' for that matter. My rôle was not to try to interpret the words according to fixed doctrines, but to be open to what could be called up from within me. Instead of wrestling with the words to discover their meaning, I had to listen with an open heart and allow the meaning to be ‘born’ in me. The medieval religious orders called this Lectio Divina—divine reading—although their religious interpretations often got in the way of this. I began to see words as being like buckets dipping down into the deep well of the unconscious and bringing into consciousness the nurture appropriate to my need at the time. No wonder Jesus said, on several occasions, ‘*He who has ears to hear, let him hear.*’ Transformation doesn’t come from passively believing that a story is factual but from having the true and personal meaning activated in the heart. It’s not about knowing, but about experiencing.

If a way can be found to the heart, the Spirit (whatever that means) can always find it. This was certainly my experience and that of many of my fellow fundamentalist Christians, though we didn’t, indeed couldn’t, recognise the full import of what was happening to us at the time. Often a passage of scripture would speak to someone about something in his or her life. In my religious hey-day the only source of such inspiration was the Bible or the books of certain reputable authors (that is, those who held the same beliefs as me). But once I had seen how words and symbols worked, I could find a rich source of meaning in virtually anything I read.

I can hear voices of protest now, asking if that isn't dangerous, and I agree it can be, but it became less dangerous as I began to discern what some might refer to as 'the voice of God'. I like to use the old His Master’s Voice logo as a metaphor for this experience. A few years ago, before the media company re-branded itself HMV, its logo was a dog sitting beside an ancient gramophone trumpet. The logo’s inference was that the sound reproduced on the company's 78 r.p.m records was of such high fidelity that the dog could recognise his master's voice.

When I got into religion I became locked into one way of hearing. Unless I heard a certain form or intonation of words or a certain kind of music, I didn't feel I was being 'religious', but this was just my ego's 'false self' at work. I could only think about religion in familiar ways. But Jesus' ministry was all about getting people to look at their religion differently. He used the phrase '*but I tell you*' eight times in Matthew's gospel. He was saying, 'You've been told it's like that, but I tell you it's like this.' The ego's response to such a paradox is to pick up stones ready to throw. The spiritual response is 'Aha!' Once my ear became attuned to the 'master's voice,' I could recognise it in the most unexpected places—in a film, on TV, in a newspaper article, a novel or a poem.

Of course, I've had to exercise honest discernment to enable this to happen and, unlike the evangelical Christian me, I never seek guidance about specific issues from scripture. It's easy to be misled. One popular story illustrates what can happen when discernment is not used. A lady of the church needed guidance about what she should do with some money. She closed her eyes, prayed for guidance, flipped open her Bible randomly and ran her finger down the page. When she opened her eyes she read, 'And he cast down the pieces of silver in the temple, and departed, and went and hanged himself.' She just *knew* that couldn't be right, so she went through the exercise again. This time she read, 'Go and do thou likewise.'

Active experience is much more important than passive knowledge. Over the years I've met many people who, like me, knew a lot about religion but, from the way they behaved, they clearly weren't experiencing much peace, love or joy. Many of them found it difficult to love others because they really didn't love themselves much. Religion was a means of dealing with their own poor self-image, as it had been mine. Jesus said it was 'by their fruits' you can know those who are true to him, not by their doctrines.

Believing uncritically that the Bible was the inerrant word of "God" had given me bed-rock certainty and that's precisely what any insecure soul needs. Even so, there can be little doubt my maturity had been retarded. It took many years before I was conscious of the issues arising out of such a belief and even more before I came to terms with them. Fortunately, I eventually grew up and came to understand faith is not about certainty, but about trust. But trust in what or in whom? Discovering a new way to think about the ultimate reality, the divine, or what we refer to as 'God', would be a much bigger challenge.

Chapter Seven

It Ain't Necessarily So

The t'ings dat yo' li'ble
To read in de Bible,
It ain't necessarily so.
George & Ira Girshwin

The God I believed in as a fundamentalist Christian had certain characteristics clearly defined in the Bible. We were all agreed the characteristics of our "God" were the only true ones. There could be no other way to think about 'Him'. If anyone defined "God" differently, theirs was obviously a different "God" from ours and therefore a false "God". You couldn't have one "God" with many conflicting characteristics, could you? This, I assumed in my ignorance, had been true from the beginning. Adam and Eve believed it and passed it on down the line right through to Jesus, to Paul and eventually, to me and my generation of churchgoers. Other people's beliefs were deviations which arose out of original sin.

Our religion was traditionally monotheistic. It was my general assumption that, since the Bible began with the creation story, monotheism had been in existence since the beginning of time. I'd never taken the trouble to research the history of religion, neither was I encouraged to do so by my elders. No one I knew had ever researched the origins and evolution of religion - I guess that would have been much too dangerous. The Bible was deemed entirely sufficient, so why make life complicated?

The Bible, I was taught, is the history of the failure of human beings and of God's working to restore them to himself. Primitive tribes and prehistoric people, we believed, were not people who had never developed, but evidence of regression from the perfection of "God" as an outcome of 'The Fall'. We quoted Romans 5:12 in support of the principle of original sin: 'Therefore, just as sin entered the world through one man [Adam], and death through sin . . . in this way death came to all people, because all sinned.' Once Adam and Eve had left the Garden of Eden it was downhill all the way. Sinfulness grew and this had a tangible effect on the length of time people lived. We noted that early in the Bible life expectancy seemed to be up to 1000 years or more. By the time of Abraham and his sons it was down to 100. Then in the Psalms life expectancy is only 70—80 if you're lucky.

With all this in mind, the way in which human thought had evolved — from animism to polytheism and finally to monotheism—never entered my mind. It became obvious to me eventually, but for as long as I was within the fold of the church, I was trapped in my paradigm. All history and pre-history had to be made to fit with the stories of the divinely-inspired Bible. The outcome, naturally, was intellectual and psychological chaos. Evolutionary Christian, Michael Dowd says that it's like a person using an ancient map on a modern SatNav. Imagine expecting to find an open savannah and finding the M5 instead! (Mind you, I understand some SatNavs are prone to such errors!)

Jews, Christians and Muslims, I eventually discovered, did not actually hold the world rights to monotheism. About 100 years before the supposed exodus of the Hebrews from Egypt, the Pharaoh, Akhenaten, had monotheistic ideas. Indeed, even at their most polytheistic, the Egyptians seem to have had a monotheistic streak. Sir E.A. Wallis Budge, referring to epithets applied to Egyptian gods collected by Dr. H. Brugsch from texts of the 18th and 19th dynasties, says, '. . . *from these we may see the ideas and beliefs of the Egyptians concerning "God" were almost identical to those of the Hebrews and Mohammedans at later periods.*' He then quotes a number of Egyptian epithets including this one:

> *'God is one and alone, and none other existeth with Him; God is the One, the One Who hath made all things.'*[11]

Had I read this in my fundamentalist days, not knowing its source, I would have been looking it up in my concordance, fully expecting to find it

11 Egyptian Religion, E.A. Wallis Budge

somewhere in the Psalms or perhaps the Prophets. Once I had discovered it was Egyptian, though, I would have probably thought it was a deception of Satan, who so deviously seeds his lies with truth. This was the kind of reasoning to which I'd resorted to maintain my fundamentalist 'faith'.

Origins

It seems probable the Hebrews acquired much of their symbolism from the Egyptians because there are some marked similarities:

- Akhenaten placed two symbolic pillars, representing strength and wisdom, at the entrance of Karnak. "God" is said to have led the children of Israel through the wilderness by a pillar of cloud by day, another of fire by night. Solomon erected two pillars (called Joachin and Boaz) before the temple; and we still talk of 'the pillars of wisdom'. In fact pillars are a common feature of most cultures of most periods of history, right from the Neolithic era onwards.
- In the version of the ten commandments that appears in Deuteronomy, "God" declares himself to be a jealous "God". According to Professor Flinders Petrie, 'The Aten was the only instance of a jealous god in Egypt.' [12]
- The Aten was Akhenaten's only "God", represented by the sun's disk.
- 'The Ark, ritually employed as a symbolic form of transport for the god Aten in ceremonies in Amarna, was used by the Jews of the Exodus to carry items associated with the divine revelation [13]
- The commission of the family of Levi to be hereditary priests in Israel, resembles the priestly families of Egypt.

But the Hebrews weren't good at monotheism. All through their history, prophets reprimanded them for their defection to 'strange gods'. Even the wise Solomon worshipped many gods and there was a period of

12 The Religion of Ancient Egypt, F. Petrie
13 Cracking the Symbol Code, Tim Wallace-Murphy

some six hundred years during which the Passover was not celebrated regularly.

Traditionally Semitic tribes thought their Gods belonged to the tribe, rather than that the tribe belonged to their "God". For Israel it was Yahweh's job to keep them out of trouble and at the top of the league. If he didn't, he was in danger of being dealt with like any other team manager and sacked. But Yahweh was a "God" of War and not much help when it came to raising crops or breeding livestock. For this job it was deemed more appropriate to importune the help of various fertility gods.

Even if it had actually been part of the Hebrew culture, full blown monotheism didn't actually arrive among the children of Abraham until the sixth century BCE, though the seeds for it had been sown two centuries earlier. I was interested to discover that Hebraic monotheism arose in the middle of what became known as 'the axial age' which lasted from 900 BCE to about 200 BCE. It was a period when a sea change took place in human thinking worldwide. Karen Armstrong says that,

> *'In four distinct regions sages, prophets and mystics began to develop traditions that have continued to nourish men and women: Hinduism, Buddhism and Jainism in the Indian subcontinent, Confucianism and Daoism in China, monotheism in the middle east and philosophical rationalism in Greece.'*[14]

In the middle of the eighth century BCE a new idea began to simmer in the minds of Judah's religious elite. Some of them began to present their patron god, Yahweh, as the one and only legitimate god, not only of Israel, but among all gods. Until then, Yahweh had been one among many. Now the many were cast as false gods, which was a radical change of thinking, though not entirely novel. The Pharaoh, Akenhaten, had proposed such a thing five hundred years earlier, but after his death Egypt immediately reverted to its polytheistic traditions.

---

14 Twelve Steps to a Compassionate Life, pp 26,27, Karen Armstrong, Bodley Head

It may be recorded in Genesis that Hebrew religion began with Abraham but the Torah wasn't actually written until the 7th and 6th century BCE, seven or eight centuries after Abraham. Formerly rulers had made records of their triumphs on clay or stone tablets and stele, but a new medium capable of keeping more detailed written records of the history of kings and peoples had swept the eastern Mediterranean and middle eastern countries: papyrus. It was at this time the Homeric sagas were also written down.

Scribes in the Northern Kingdom of Israel had written a version of their history calling their god, Elohim. The scribes of Judah had written their version calling their god, Yahweh. When Israel's Northern Kingdom was destroyed and its ruling classes taken into captivity by Assyria, many people fled to Jerusalem and that is how their historical books, including the oracles of the Northern Kingdom prophets, Hosea and Amos, found their way into the Jewish archives. There they were held alongside the Jewish version. Modern experts have labelled these two documents J, for Yahweh, and E, for Elohim.[15] These were combined, edited and material added to produce the original version of the Torah.

Additional material should not be thought of as forgery, even though by modern standards it would be thought of as such. In those days it was a sincere attempt to make sense of what was happening. In every culture under the sun there had been a mythic period when people expressed their experience of the mysteries of existence in terms of stories describing outlandish creatures and supernatural phenomena. Initially these were recounted orally by poets and shamans and nuanced according to changes in culture. As rational thought came to prominence and factual record keeping was established, history and myth were woven together. Yet still the important thing was not in recording an accurate record, as we would today, but in conveying the meaning of an experience. Thus the captives in Babylon could take great comfort from the stories of the Exodus. Indeed, deriving meaning from this story has helped many in slavery or

15 The Bible, Karen Armstrong, p14, Grove Press.

imprisonment in modern times. A story doesn't have to be factual to be meaningful.

The description of the Bible's beginning is found in 2 Kings 22:8 where we read that Hilkiah the high priest found a book during the rebuilding of the temple which he presented to King Josiah. This newly discovered book is widely thought to have been the core of Deuteronomy[16], though whether it was 'found' or actually written then we cannot be sure. Certainly neither the text of 'J' or 'E' contained the law of Moses.[17] The Torah, the first five books of the Bible, was put together using various source-texts by a group of people known as the 'Deuteronomists'. To this was added both the J and E versions of the histories. The whole work became known as the Tanekh, the equivalent of the Christian Old Testament. However, the Tanekh had little effect on the people of Judea until the Babylonian captivity. In Babylon it would come to have an enormous influence.

Nebuchadnezzar overthrew Jerusalem in about 587 BCE and the elite of Israel were carried off to Babylon. Simultaneously, or maybe as a result of this event, a new religious movement arose among Jewish prophets—the 'Yahweh Alone' movement. The prophets told the people that the captivity had not resulted from Yahweh's desertion of *them*. It was a punishment for their desertion of *Him*. The solution was obvious: they must obey the law of Yahweh and turn away from any other gods.

Whereas the exiles had no shrine, for that could only be in Jerusalem, they did have a new book of law and this became the focus of their religious lives. The text of the law became a new shrine[18] and maybe this reliance on a text laid the foundations for future fundamentalism in all the Levantine faiths, including my own. As Christians, we had supported our arguments of inerrancy with Old Testament quotations about 'The Word of the Lord', which, in my ignorance, I'd assumed to refer to the Bible.

It became apparent to me that the motive for producing the book which would become the Old Testament was not altogether divine but largely political. In Babylon many of the captive Jews had risen to places of

16 Cosmos, Chaos and the World to Come, Norman Cohn, Yale University Press.

17 The Bible, Karen Armstrong, p17, Grove Press.

18 The Battle for God, Karen Armstrong, Harper Collins

authority in Nebuchadnezzar's court, as the story of Daniel confirms. Although a life of captivity had its downs, many found it had considerable ups. Within a generation the captives were given considerable freedom. They built their own houses in their own villages, set up businesses and could even be found in the higher echelons of government. Far from 'weeping beside the waters', as the psalmist has it, many people were comfortably settled. For instance, it is said that the Greek mathematician, Pythagoras, had been taken into slavery from Egypt at this time and remained captive for ten years. Yet when offered his freedom, he remained another ten years to study mathematics.

What we call 'the captivity' had actually taken place in several waves over a period of 40 years; therefore a time came when some mature people had been born in captivity and had never even seen Jerusalem. Older folks only remembered Jerusalem in ruins and the deprivations they endured in the lead up to the first captivity. There wasn't much incentive to return to their shattered home city. Therefore the new History of Israel was produced to overcome people's reluctance to obey the call of the prophets to return to Jerusalem. It was designed to make them feel special—God's chosen people in fact. The ploy was relatively successful. Some people returned to the city and others contributed money so Jerusalem could be restored to its former glory—although it never was.

What is not commonly known among members of the Levantine faiths that arose out of Judaism is that a large swathe of their theology is derived from the influence of the Persian religion, Zoroastrianism. This Zoroastrian influence had certainly never been brought to my attention, a serious deficit considering that so much Biblical mythology had come from it. As a Christian I didn't know much about the religion other than that it figured in my book of heresies. The book listed ancient sects such as Manicheism and Gnosticism, along with modern ones like the Church of Jesus Christ of Latter-Day Saints (Mormonism) and Jehovah's Witnesses. I hadn't bothered to read the references to Zoroastrians in my book, since I hadn't met any. If I did come into contact with any, I knew just where to get the information that would help me show them how wrong they were and convert them to Jesus.

The Zoroastrians among whom the captives lived also believed in one "God", Ahura Mazda, the god of light. But they also believed in an antithetical being called Angra Mainyu. This being was responsible for all evil including demonic possession, which led to sickness and disease. He was constantly trying to thwart the perfect creation of Ahura Mazda. Zoroastrian mythology described a Day of the Lord, when Ahura Mazda would send his servant, the Sayoshant, to deliver the world from evil. He would be born of a virgin and come to judge the people of the earth, dividing them like a shepherd divides his flock, black sheep to the left, white sheep to the right. Those who had not obeyed the law of Ahura Mazda would be cast into a fiery abyss of molten metal, where they would suffer until the end of the era. Then the dead would be resurrected and an earthly perfection restored. Sounds familiar?

Up to this point in their history the Jews had no concept of heaven and hell, no angels and no devil. For them the afterlife was an eternity in Sheol, a colourless place where the dead dwelt. Their only hope was to raise children, preferably sons, who would take on the family business and leave their parents a good name among their neighbours. The Zoroastrians changed all that.

Prophetic writing had long been a feature of Jewish religion. Ezekiel had written strange and highly symbolic visions during his ministry at the beginning of the fifth century BCE. This style of prophecy was continued among Jews, who by now had spread themselves in small communities throughout the Persian empire.

A number of prophetic works have come down to us from this era, notably 1 Enoch, compiled between 300 BCE and 100 AD, and the book of Jubilees, composed between 175 and 140 BCE. They are written in a highly symbolic style known as 'apocalyptic', a Greek word meaning 'an unveiling', and although they are very Jewish, the influence of Zoroastrianism is plain. The concepts they hold were intended to embolden a people who were being cruelly oppressed, as had been the people in the days of Isaiah, Jeremiah and Daniel. The first post-captivity oppressor was Antiochus of Syria, who tried to stamp out Judaism, and it is to him that many of the symbols used by the prophets refer. Later, of course, came the Romans.

The Jewish apocalypses include predictions of the end time including, the coming of a saviour, judgement, resurrection of the dead and a final completion of the age by "God". Like later Christian apocalyptic teaching, they expected the 'Day of the Lord' to be imminent, as a response to the contemporary suffering of the people. Even in the days of Jesus the canon of the Tanekh had not been finalised, but that was a mere formality, for there was agreement among the Rabbis about which books were authoritative and which were 'non-canonical', and Enoch and Jubilees were among the latter. Even so, the Rabbis weren't averse to using non-canonical books including these. It is clear, therefore, that the foundation for the Christian concepts of heaven, hell, Satan, angels, the Messiah, the virgin birth and the judgement of the last days had been firmly established well before Jesus was born. And it came from material that would never be recognised as authoritative, either by Jewish Rabbis or, later, by the Church Fathers.

When the Persian emperor Cyrus decided to send the captives back to Judah to rebuild the temple in Jerusalem, they reached an obvious conclusion. Having returned to the worship of Yahweh exclusively, as the prophets had declared, He had turned to them and rewarded them. One can imagine why a similar euphoria gripped some Jews when they were given Israel as a homeland in 1948, and during the 1967 Six-day War and its aftermath. Certainly we fundamentalist Christians saw these events as evidence of 'the hand of God' fulfilling prophecy. Anything which seems to corroborate the belief of the fundamentalist is seized upon with some alacrity. Even today there are conservative Christians who will not support any protests against Israeli oppression of the Palestinians, because they believe that the land they occupy was given to the Jews by "God". (Elizabeth jokes, if "God" had really wanted to give them a wonderful land to live in, surely he would have given them Italy!)

So, as an historical document the Old Testament is like an autobiography, which may be more about what ought to have happened, than what actually did. Its history, though remarkably accurate in places, is heavily laced with political ambition and, as has been the tradition of human kind, its heroes have practically all been mythologized. Perhaps, more importantly, material has been clearly imported from those amongst whom the Hebrew tribes had their existence: Egypt, Canaan, Babylon and Persia.

The aftershocks of the tectonic shift in consciousness that took place during the 'axial age' continue to this day. They influenced the rise of Christianity and Islam and rumble along the fault lines between modern Israel and Palestine, among Middle Eastern terrorist groups and Christian fundamentalists trying to influence Western politics.

Chapter Eight

The God I Left Behind

As a fundamentalist Christian I got my concept of "God" from the Bible as filtered by my church. My view was:

- He is male.
- He exists in three persons: Father, Son and Holy Spirit.
- He lives in another dimension of existence called Heaven.
- He created the world and everything in it by miraculous intervention.
- He has a purpose for those who believe in him.
- He continues to intervene in the world by producing miracles, largely in answer
  to the prayers of believers.

I guess most Jews, Muslims, Christians and Zoroastrians would subscribe to such characteristics as these, no matter to what denomination or sect they belong. Most atheists would also agree these are the characteristics of the "God" in which they don't believe.

He is Male (Of course *He* is!)

In an age where 'equality' is the mantra chanted in every corner of government and business, it is difficult to justify the idea of an exclusively male "God". Many believers go to considerable lengths to show that "God" is beyond maleness and femaleness. Even so most of them consistently refer to a 'Him', call him 'Father' (if they're Christians), speak to a 'him' in prayer and ascribe many aggressive characteristics of maleness to him. I've even found myself letting slip a 'Him' in unguarded moments. It's a difficult habit to break.

Without exception, all the Levantine religions (Judaism, Christianity and Islam) are heavily weighted towards the dominance of the male. This is amply evidenced in the religious and social behaviour observable among followers of these religions, no matter what the complexion of individual beliefs. The scriptures which make up the Hindu Vedas, Buddhist scripture and those of the Taoists, also express their themes in predominantly male terms. Yet it is one thing for theologians to argue that "God" has no sexual organs; quite another to couch all references to "God" as 'Him'. Worse, to put women into an inferior rôle. The ongoing arguments in the Church of England over whether women should become priests or bishops illustrate the problems that arise from such paradigms.

Most of the stories in the Old Testament originated in the Bronze Age. It was a stage in social evolution when patrist attitudes began to dominate. Around 3000 BC there had been a shift in climate which caused the Sahara Desert to migrate further north. The current theory is that when people began farming they developed the new idea of ownership. Hunter/gatherers have little or no such concept. Ownership means you may have to defend and protect your possessions and so the rôle of warrior developed. By the early Bronze age we see the first defensive structures. Then there came a climate change. The North African desert began to move northward. The land could no no longer sustain these people so they went seeking for new territory. The trouble was that the world population had expanded and there wasn't much vacant territory within easy reach. So the migrating people were forced to turn the weapons they'd used for hunting into weapons of war and take land by force. The warrior culture that grew out of this was predominantly patristic and women became regarded as possessions. The concept of the male god supplanted the concept of the female god of earlier generations.

The first book of the Bible epitomises the struggle between these two concepts. In the first of the two creation stories, Eve is made from Adam's rib. There is a romantic view, often trotted out by apologists, that this signifies she came from near his heart but it doesn't excuse the implication that the Adam was 'mother' first, making Eve's rôle subservient to his. Later "God" makes promises to Abraham about his 'seed', either revealing God's ignorance of gynaecology or the desire of the authors to show it was from the male that life came. Eve was merely the growbag in which the seed was planted!

It is quite clear the authors of Genesis thought of "God" as a dominant male. He was so human-like he needed to 'walk in the garden in the cool of the day' (Genesis 3:8). (Can you imagine it — God breaking into a sweat?) Far from man being created in God's image (Genesis 1:26), it seems, this god had been created in man's image and bears all the behavioural characteristics of the male human being. For instance:

- He is a jealous god (Exodus 20:25).
- He uses violence to achieve his ends (Exodus 17:14,15) (Qu'ran, TheFamily of Imran, 3.167)
- He glories in physical strength (Nehemiah 1:10) (Qu'ran, The Women, 4.84)
- He is homophobic (Leviticus 20:13) (Qu'ran, The Ant, 27.55) (Romans 1:26
- He treats women as inferior to men (Genesis 2:18) (Qu'ran, The Cow, 2.282) (1 Corinthians 14:35)

It is belief in this kind of god, and the understanding of self that arises naturally from it that has been the cause of so much violence down the centuries. The wars perpetrated by Muslim leaders in the several hundred years of Islamic expansion, the crusades and inquisitions by Christians, civil wars in England and France, the troubles of Northern Ireland, inter-faith violence in the Balkans and the continuing Israeli-Palestinian conflict. I suggest these are, at least an indirect, and often a direct consequence of a mindset that justifies violence because of a belief in a male god capable of vindictiveness and anger. It's a mindset that seems to say, 'If "God" uses violence to overcome His enemies, it must be OK for me to behave like that too.'

Like the notorious American evangelist Pat Robertson, many of us fundamentalist Christians believed that even natural disasters could be God's punishment on wicked people. The sufferings of the people in the

2009 Haitian earthquake, according to Robertson, was because of their wickedness. For fundamentalists, there are plenty of verses in the Bible to support such an argument—Noah's flood, and Sodom and Gomorrah, for instance. Such beliefs were common among Bronze Age cultures who knew nothing of geology or meteorology. Such are the depths of ignorance to which modern fundamentalism ultimately leads. It's a downward spiral. In order to justify one concept you have to create another and another, until you have built, between you and the truth, a barrier so strong nothing can penetrate it.

He exists in three persons: Father, Son and Holy Spirit.
The Catholic Encyclopedia gives as good a definition of the trinity as any:

> *'The Trinity is the term employed to signify the central doctrine of the Christian religion—the truth that in the unity of the Godhead there are Three Persons, the Father, the Son, and the Holy Spirit, these Three Persons being truly distinct one from another.*
>
> *'Thus, in the words of the Athanasian Creed: 'the Father is God, the Son is God, and the Holy Spirit is God, and yet there are not three Gods but one God.' In this Trinity of Persons the Son is begotten of the Father by an eternal generation, and the Holy Spirit proceeds by an eternal procession from the Father and the Son. Yet, notwithstanding this difference as to origin, the Persons are co-eternal and co-equal: all alike are uncreated and omnipotent. This, the Church teaches, is the revelation regarding God's nature which Jesus Christ, the Son of God, came upon earth to deliver to the world: and which she proposes to man as the foundation of her whole dogmatic system.'*

The so-called "church fathers", argued about the nature of "God" for some three centuries before deciding on a formula. This doctrine has generally stuck fast and was not thrown out during the reformation. My guess is that this was because at its heart lies a mystical, rather than theological idea. But what emerged from it was a clearly established doctrine that Jesus is to be considered co-equal with "God".

All this became necessary to 'tidy up' the loose ends left by the Bible and, by making Jesus into part of the Godhead, it reinforced the authority of the church—at least in the minds of the Christian theocracy. Might it have been from deep sincerity in this doctrine that many of the atrocities perpetrated by the church arose? I've often thought that if I had believed sincerely that my loved ones would burn in hell for eternity because they didn't believe that Jesus, as "God", had died for their sins, I'd have been in tears pleading daily for them to repent. Maybe some medieval believers were more sincere than me. In their perverted way they at least tried to torture people into belief, thinking that giving them a taste of hell would help them avoid the real thing. I did nothing but feel rejection because others wouldn't believe about Jesus the same things I did.

He lives in another dimension of existence called Heaven

The writers of the Bible thought the cosmos was constructed of three parts: heaven, earth and hell (or sheol). "God" dwelt in heaven which is above (Job 22:12) and made things happen on the earth below (Psalm 135:6,7). Beneath the earth was sheol or hell, which was originally, not a place of fire, but simply a rather boring place where the dead went. As I pointed out in the previous chapter, the kind of heaven we imagine and hell were among concepts that developed out of the Jewish brush with the Zoroastrians in Babylon.

As the concept of eternal punishment developed, it became the place where the disobedient went (Luke 16:19-31). This cosmology was central to religious belief right up to Galileo (1564 - 1642) and beyond. It provided generations of religious leaders with an extremely potent control mechanism. Even as a 20th Century fundamentalist I retained vestiges of such thinking, which shaped my concept of the cosmos.

With the eventual realisation that Galileo was right and the earth did go around the sun, the church had to begin revising its cosmology. It isn't possible to suggest the writers of the Bible were consistently using metaphor, because they weren't. It is quite clear the fifth century Deuteronomists, were writing, or perhaps redacting, what they regarded as history. Their main aim was not to present symbolic revelation. It was to establish the Jewish claim on Jerusalem and encourage the captives to return. They really weren't worried about the difference between fact and myth.

Nevertheless symbolism is found everywhere in the Bible and for the writers and redactors everything had both a temporal and a symbolic aspect, and it was possible for the people of that era to gain understanding from either. It really didn't matter whether a story was factually reliable, meaning could be derived from its symbolic aspect.

Since the so-called Enlightenment, modernist thinkers have always had to distinguish between the temporal and the symbolic. It seems to me, this is what helped we fundamentalists to get ourselves into such a fix. We could understand that some passages contained symbolism but in addition, we expected that the base story had to be factual or the Bible was a lie. If the writers of the biblical books spoke 'according to their understanding at the time', as it was explained to me, then how could it be 'the infallibly inspired word of God'? Surely He knew that their concept of the cosmos was incorrect, so why did he not inspire them with the truth? If Jesus is truly "God" why didn't He know all this business about the location of heaven and hell wasn't true? The account of his ascension into heaven from the Mount of Olives perpetuates this three-layered view of the cosmos. Jesus physically ascended into heaven according Matthew. According to Paul he's still there waiting to physically return. But, in a physical body, as he reportedly went to some lengths to show Thomas he had, even travelling at the speed of light, he would not have yet left our galaxy! It seems such a pity to have to believe as factual such an impossible story, when the symbolic aspect alone contains such rich spiritual truth.

Paul's teaching about the second coming of Jesus was based on this cosmic view and was clearly derived from the Jewish apocalyptic books of 1 Enoch and Jubilees. He says:

'For the Lord himself shall descend from heaven with a shout, with the voice of the archangel, and with the trump of "God": and the dead in Christ shall rise first: Then we which are alive and remain shall be caught up together with them in the clouds, to meet the Lord in the air: and so shall we ever be with the Lord.'[19]

Clearly, Paul expected, as the Jews a century or two before, that he and his flock would see this event for he says, 'we which are alive and remain'. This is another thing fundamentalists have had to get around and sometimes the rationalisation has been extreme. Every now and again, an influential believer would arise (usually in America) who would claim Jesus was coming on a given day. His followers (and it was usually men who did this) would go into a mountain somewhere to await the Lord's return. They would hang around for a day or two after the forecast date, just in case the calculation had been slightly out, then go home to rationalise the non-event. Thus, the second coming of Jesus has been regularly predicted each turn of a century, at the turn of each millennium and often at many other 'divinely inspired' dates in between.

I have to say neither the Brethren nor the Charismatics went this far. We'd quote Matthew 24:36 which says no one, not even the Son of God, knows when the last day will appear. But we still thought news of wars and rumours of wars, earthquakes, famines and pestilences and the restoration of the State of Israel in Palestine were all the precursors of the Second Coming. Conflicts in Israel and predictions in Revelation concerning the Beast, (for us the Roman Catholic Church) all seemed to confirm our view that the return of Jesus was imminent. Soon we would 'ascend to meet him in the skies'.

He created the world and all that's in it by miraculous intervention

We were 'creationists', believing that "God" literally created the world in six days as set out in the first chapter of Genesis. To us evolution was an invention of the Devil. Not only did the brothers and sisters of the Gospel Hall believe this, but many well-educated writers of intellectual Christian

19 1 Thessalonians 4:16,17

tomes and not a few Christians who were scientists believed it too. Who was I to disagree? High intellect doesn't predispose people to rationality, it seems. I needed to believe creation in order to show that the Bible is the 'inspired Word of God' and therefore accurate, and above all dependable, in every detail. Creationism is a sort of 'reverse engineering'. You start with a concept you accept as fact, then work your way back to prove it to be true. Unlike a real scientific hypothesis, the only evidence you can come up with is the supposition that Bible is 'His inerrant word'. You have to ignore all the evidence to the contrary. Indeed, faith was all about believing in impossible things. The more impossible it seemed, the more ardently I believed it. It was my badge of honour.

The idea of 'intelligent design', which has been growing in popularity among Christian believers, is just one step removed from creationism. It was developed in America, some time after my departure from fundamentalism, to overcome the objection to teaching creationism in schools. It suggests there is an intelligence behind creation without defining it specifically as "God". So far so good. However, adherents to this concept do envisage the Christian "God" as being the intelligent force behind the design, if not the production process. This seems to make "God" more like a design engineer than a creator. Both creation by direct intervention and creation by intelligent design arise from a belief that there is an entity we call "God", who intervenes from outside the physical universe to make things happen. But, as I observed with an open mind the haphazard (biologists say 'random') way in which creatures and plants evolve, it became more and more difficult to believe in that kind of direct intervention by a loving "God". The difficulty of holding on to such a concept in the light of modern science and observation of nature may be one of the reasons why so many have turned away from religion. If such a proposition is true, "God" executes his creativity in a most unfair, unequal and seemingly unintelligent way. There had to be another answer to the problem of creation and I shall address this in the next chapter.

He has a purpose for those who believe in him

Many Christians view their individual purpose as being wrapped up with 'obedience to God's will', 'furthering the Gospel' or 'being prepared for His second coming'. Muslims also believe they can only please Allah by strict observance of rituals. Similarly Jews believe their purpose to be obedient in all things to the law as given in the Torah. As a Christian, I claimed I was no longer under law[20]. However, my behaviour, in relation to 'seeking God's will', demonstrated I was still fearful of upsetting my father-god. In effect, I was as law-observing as any of the other Levantine believers. I recognise this attitude among many Christians, especially those who brand themselves 'evangelicals'. As a result of such legalism, I lost much spontaneity of life and became geared to living out my strict religious beliefs, rather than being a natural human being. The fear of not doing 'His will' and the associated guilt had a harmful effect on both my personal conduct and my health. I would often procrastinate over simple things, like whether to attend a meeting or not, and such worrying generated a lot of stomach acid. Our medicine chest was full of stomach medicines and I made regular trips to the doctor with duodenal pain.

Now liberated from such attitudes, I realise I am uniquely fitted to fulfil certain rôles and functions I encounter on my path. To fulfil these rôles and functions all I need is an awareness of myself and of others, and a relationship with the Presence I find in silence. In this there arises an 'enabling' and everything then falls into place.

He continues to intervene in the world by producing miracles largely in answer to the prayers of believers.

My prayer life was governed by the belief that "God" intervenes. I took before Him a shopping list of requests, hoping they would be answered. My main problem was that "God" didn't answer most prayers. Those he did were rarely answered in the way I'd expected. Indeed, an article in the *New York Times* of 31st March 2006, confirmed that ten scientifically reliable research projects into the efficacy of prayer for hospital patients

20 Romans 6:14

delivered inconsistent results. There seems to be no certain scientific evidence that prayer works as we expect it to. As a fundamentalist Christian I'd have waved that evidence aside, feeling that it was dishonourable not to trust "God" and rationalise the outcomes as His will, which is far above my understanding.

In the American novel, *The Cold Sassy Tree*, by Olive Ann Burns, Will Tweedy's Grandpa asks some important questions which sum up our predicament about prayer: 'If'n you give God the credit when somebody don't die, you go'n blame Him when they do die? Call it His will?' Then he adds, 'Ever noticed we git well all the time and don't die but once't?'

When my prayers weren't answered, I'd descend into rationalism. I'd say simply, 'It wasn't His will' or I'd quote the old hymn: 'God works in a mysterious way, His wonders to perform'. Nowadays, when I hear this sort of rationalism expressed, it makes me want to shout a rather rude word.

If I was not to spend my life rationalising my experiences of life so they could come within the scope of my concept of "God", I had to find a different concept, not only of prayer but of God. I needed one which would tie in with what I could see going on around me, one which could be verified in my experience, not in my dogma.

Part III:

A New World

> *'We do not need a new religion or a new Bible. We need a new experience—a new feeling of what it is to be 'I'.'* Alan Watts

It's common for each of us to consider life as a journey. It may not seem so at the time of living it, but when we look back we see the contours of a great country through which we've travelled, suffered, rejoiced and endured. So I begin Part III with an examination of the traditional hero's journey of mythology, one in which the hero goes out to obtain a boon for mankind. This lays a foundation for what may be thought of as the boon of my own journey, which is the discovery of my own True Self, the subject of Chapters 10, 11and 12.

In this section I reflect on the spiritual issues which have undoubtedly shaped my life, revisiting concepts of "God", the Bible and Jesus, and seeing the relationship of science to the future of spiritual thought and living. I conclude with an appraisal of how humanity got into the mess we're in and some things we might individually do about it.

Chapter Nine

The Spiritual Journey

Read as an historical document the Bible is of academic interest. Read as mythology it is rich in symbolism and can draw the reader into a transcendent experience. The problem with fundamentalism is that it tries to make the Bible both an historical and mythological record. This sets up a conflict between the logical left brain, which is trying to make rational sense out of everything, and the intuitive right brain which seeks, not knowledge, but experience. There is nothing wrong with reading the Bible as an historical document. As such it is fascinating. But you can't do that at the same time as reading it as mythology—not if you want to get the full benefit of what the mythology is saying. I had to learn to read the Bible in a completely new way.

Mythological stories are full of tales of adventure and discovery. Like other symbolic media they can be read on a number of levels. At one level they may represent meaning for a tribe or family. At another, they may generate meaning about a given situation in an individual's life. They often represent a generic journey of self-discovery, applicable to everyone. From his study of thousands of mythological stories, comparative mythologist Joseph Campbell identified a number of stages in the spiritual journey [21]:

The Call
Detachment or withdrawal
Crossing the threshold
Obtaining the boon
The return.

---

21 The Hero with a Thousand Faces, Joseph Campbell, Paladin

The typical five-stage 'hero' story of ancient mythology, of which there are many in the Bible, may best be illustrated by the Greek story of Jason and the Golden Fleece: [22] Jason, the son of King Aeson, the late ruler of Ioicus, a city in Thessaly, was tricked into going on his heroic journey by his uncle Pelias. His uncle had been given the throne by Jason's father until Jason should reach the age of majority. Pelias suggested that Jason should go in search of the golden fleece which was known to be held in Colchis, guarded by a sleepless dragon. He reasoned that, since it was most unlikely that Jason would ever return, he would be able to keep the throne.

Jason commissioned Argos to build a great boat, and recruited fifty of the most able men to row it. They called it the Argo, after her builder. On their journey to Colchis they put into Thrace where Jason was given instructions about the rest of the journey by a sage called Phineas. It is common to hero myths that the hero meets 'helpers' of various kinds, seemingly by accident, but sometimes such helpers are gods in disguise.

At the entrance to the Euxine Sea Jason encountered his first challenge. The ship had to pass between two floating islands, called the Symplegades, or Clashing Rocks. These rocks had a nasty habit of clashing together in the swell before a ship could get through to the other side, but Phineas had given Jason instructions on how to achieve a safe passage by using a dove to precede them. As they approach the clashing rocks, Jason released the dove which flew between the islands so that they clashed together. As they began to withdraw again, Jason sailed his ship through the gap before they could begin coming together again, and so they passed safely through. A kind of Moses and the Red Sea in reverse.

On arrival at Colchis, the King, Ætes, welcomed them and agreed that Jason could have the fleece provided he could yoke two bulls to a plough. Sounds easy enough but Jason soon found that the bulls had brazen feet and breathed fire. And there was another challenge. He had to plough a field with the two unruly bulls then sow the teeth of a dead dragon which, it was known, would immediately spring up as an army of soldiers and

22 The myth of Jason evolved over centuries so there are many versions.

attack him. In an act of supreme faith Jason accepted the challenge but, during the time of preparation, he managed secretly to marry King Ætes' daughter, Medea, who gave him a charm to protect him.

At the appointed day a crowd gathered at the Grove of Mars and trembled as the mighty bulls rushed in, scorching the earth as they went and making a mighty roaring sound like that of a furnace. To the amazement of the onlookers, Jason calmed the bulls with his voice, patted their necks and slipped a yoke upon them. He ploughed the field and sowed the dragon's teeth. Everyone waited with bated breath. They didn't need to wait long, for, as expected, the teeth quickly turned into an army of soldiers who immediately rushed upon Jason. At first he managed to keep them at bay with his sword and shield, but quickly realised they would soon overwhelm him. He then threw among them the charmed stone that Medea had given him, whereupon, each desperate to retrieve the stone, they fell on one another and all soon lay dead.

King Ætes said he would give Jason the golden fleece the next day. However, that evening, he was filled with rage and swore to kill Jason and his men during the night. Medea, hearing of it, went straight to Jason and led him to where the fleece was guarded by the sleepless dragon. She had prepared a potion which caused the dragon to sleep, and Jason took the fleece and Medea with all his men, safely back to Thessaly.

The call

It is quite common for mythical heroes to begin their journeys, like Jason, as a result of trickery or by accident. Remember the story of Joseph and his coat of many colours, sold into Egypt by his brothers. As for the hero, so for us. Often an unexpected event or circumstance makes us think about who we are, what we're about and where we're headed. It's not always a burning bush, a direct invitation on the shores of Galilee, or a light on the Damascus road that does this.

For me it was a series of educational wrong-roads and redundancy; for others it may be the death of a loved one, a chance meeting or reading a passage from a book. The call could come from a sentence snatched in passing from a radio programme, something a child says or a long forgotten poem suddenly recalled. It is not necessarily 'the voice of God' but the voice of the individual unconscious, informing the conscious mind of a need. Although manifesting itself in the conscious, reasoning mind, it arises out of the unconscious by way of intuition. For some it may even arise out of what Jung calls the 'collective unconscious'; the race memory or cultural mind which we have inherited by tradition or even genetically.

Jung's view was that there exists a subliminal level of consciousness that is common to all in a society and inherited from the experiences and habits of ancestors. Recent work in the field of epigenetics is demonstrating that this is perhaps more deeply so than even Jung could imagine. We now know that memory can be passed on genetically. For instance, a larger percentage than is normal for the population as a whole, of those who are descended from people who have suffered starvation, experience eating disorders. Joseph Campbell says,

> *'I am more and more convinced that there is a plane of consciousness that we are all sharing, and that the brain is a limiting machine that pulls it in.'*[23]

For most of us the call to the hero's journey is a call to greater spiritual consciousness. For some it is a call which will demand great sacrifices to obtain a boon for all the people of his or her community. Diarmuid Ó Murchú, basing his ideas on research in the early 1980s by James Fowler [24], consciously or unconsciously follows roughly the steps shown by Campbell. He describes six common experiences [25] and the first one relates very closely to Campbell's mythic 'call'.

> *'There is an awakening stage which can be triggered off by a whole range of events or experiences, usually related to questions of meaning or lack of it, in one's daily life. Common experience*

23 The Joseph Campbell Companion, Edited by Diane K. Osbon, Harper Perenial
24 Stages of Faith, James Fowler, Harpur and Row
25 Reclaiming Spirituality pp 10-12, Diarmud Ó Murchú, Crossroad

suggests that there is no conscious religious or spiritual awareness at this stage.'

We hear much about the 'seven year itch' and 'mid-life crisis' which may be an expression of this sense of need. Such calls may come more than once in lifetime, but the danger of refusing a call is that it may never come again. For some, when the call comes, a refusal can lead to psychic disturbance or worse, complete mental breakdown. The call is a warning that the conscious and unconscious are out of kilter—they are conflicted.

I should make clear that whereas in the myths the call usually comes from outside the hero, it symbolises something that operates within the individual psyche. However, it is not supernatural, but psychological. That doesn't mean that there is no mystical element to it, because the reason for the call is seldom to do with the needs of the hero, but those of the people around him or her.

A demonstration of the results of a refusal to a call may be the great artist whose personal life is a total mess. Part of the psyche is in touch with an ineffable reality which inspires great pictures, poems, music or writing. Jung infers that this too is an experience of being in touch with the 'collective unconscious'. Such individuals are equipped to give expression to underlying ideas and feelings found in the needs of a particular culture at a particular time. However, another part of the dysfunctional artist is not controlled by intuitive or logical intelligence of the upper brain, but by the reptilian and mammalian urges of the lower brain. We can see how this deeply affects individuals by examining the lives of such people as Dylan Thomas, Ludwig van Beethoven and Virginia Wolf. They were unable to integrate their artistic experience with their lives. They remained incongruent personalities whose self-image did not match their true selves. Such mental health problems can, nowadays, often be alleviated with cognitive therapy. Their causes can be many but, I suggest, the root problem is an inability of people to discover their True Selves.

The initial spiritual struggle as a result of the call is often between desire and fear, and this is well illustrated in the Bhagavad Gita. In this book Arjuna argues with his charioteer, the god Krishna, about whether to enter the battle against his relatives. It is echoed in the Bible where Jacob wrestles with "God" in Genesis 32 and in the New Testament when Jesus is tempted in the wilderness. Jung wrote extensively of the personal internal battle that took place when he was 'called' to break with Freud. It's not always easy to respond to the call when it comes, because you instinctively know that your life and your relationships will never be the same again. (I experienced something similar when I left The Religious Society of Friends)

But it is essential that the hero takes the right journey to achieve the right purpose for the right reason. Campbell illustrates this with an illustration from the 12th century story of the Quest for the Holy Grail. When the knights of the Round Table set out on their quest they very soon came to a dense wood. They found they had to split up and each find a way through. Campbell says that if you find a path don't take it, it's not yours. It's someone else's. You have to cut your own way through. (So sharpen your machete!)

Realisation that one is being 'called' to a different level of consciousness is the second stage of the process of developing self-awareness. Once you've discovered who you are, then you have to begin to realise how you must live out who you are. This often happens around midlife. By then some people have realised that the 'false self' they've developed is not truly the person they are. That began to happen to me when, at the age of thirty three, I discovered I was capable of work at university graduate level. Sadly, a substantial proportion of the population never hears the call, and so continue to perpetuate the lie and never find their true selves. But those who hear the call have a choice: respond or not. Whatever is chosen will bring a certain amount of disruption, for if you say yes, then radical changes will become necessary. If you say no you will have to live with regret for the rest of your life, which has long term consequences for both health, mental and physical and happiness.

It's important to realise that there may be many 'calls' in one's life and each poses a different challenge. Hopefully, with experience, one becomes better at taking up that challenge; learning more and more to rest in the mystery of that which leads one forth.

Detachment or Withdraw

In India, there has been a tradition that some men, having raised their families, leave their home in the capable hands of the eldest son and detach themselves physically from the family to meditate in the forest. Usually this detachment was a matter of gradual relinquishment but sometimes it was a sudden decision in response to an unexpected event (perhaps the death of someone close). The gradual detachment was preferred. However, it had to be detachment. It was not the done thing to write home from the Ashram every week saying that you were fine and asking for news of the family. Commitment had to be complete.

For most of us the detachment or withdrawal doesn't have to be physical, moving house or even changing religion, but it must be a mental detachment and it needs to be complete. You begin to see things differently. Things you valued seem tawdry and uninteresting now. Things, of which you were once unaware or that you ignored, seem to assume great relevance. This is what the New Testament writers called 'metanoia', a change of mind or in religious parlance, repentance.

Ó Murchú says that 'the call':

> *'. . . is often followed by a stage of internal confusion, which may also precede the awakening already referred to. People doubt their own experience; might try to suppress it or rationalise it; might try to explore it secretly; feelings of anger or rage may arise (aimed at*
> *oneself, the religious culture or 'God'). If the confusion persists, it*

may become deeply disturbing and even disorienting in daily life.'[26]

Borders are often dangerous places and when you arrive at a mental border, you are tempted to hold back, to stay within the comfort zone. The stage is one of brooding, gathering courage, preparing for the consequences. But whether detachment is gradual or sudden, it remains essential. I recognise it as a phase of waiting, knowing that action must be taken and trying to be aware of the right moment. The early stage is a period of uncertainty, even agony. The late stage is, for me, a stage of great inner peace. I just knew that each change, initiated by my callings, would be the right thing—changing my job, divorcing, moving to a new location, buying a house, leaving the Quakers. It was simply that I felt an inner peace about what I knew was inevitable.

Crossing the Threshold :

Of this stage in the journey, Campbell says:

> *'The call is to leave a certain social situation, move into your own loneliness and find the jewel, the centre that's impossible to find when you're socially engaged. You are thrown off-centre, and when you feel off-centre it's time to go. This is the departure when the hero feels that something has been lost and goes to find it. You cross the threshold into a new life. It's a dangerous adventure, because you are moving out of the sphere of knowledge of you and your community.'*

In the hero myths, the border is often guarded by one or more great monsters, perhaps a dragon or two. These are the 'guardians of the way' and, according to Campbell, each of the dragon's scales has written upon it 'thou shalt'. Up to this point, it is possible that your whole life has been governed by a sense of duty, responsibility or obligation. You're about to move out of this sphere and there are suddenly so many things you find

26 Reclaiming Spirituality, Diarmuid O'Murchu, Crossroads

that need to be done, so many loose ends that need tidying up. The first challenge the hero has to meet is to find a way around the dragon, either by slaying it or tricking it. This doesn't necessarily mean that you abandon your duties, responsibilities or obligations (for example, get divorced and put the kids in care), but that your attitudes are about to undergo a radical change. Therefore, so is the way in which, from now on, you will fulfil your rôle on every front. Such a change of mind is the first challenge of your spiritual journey. The guardian of the frontier that you must overcome is fear. While your friends are still in the boat, and the storm of uncertainty rages around you, it is you, because of the intuitive call, who has to step out and walk on water.

In *The Power of Myth*, Joseph Campbell relates a mythological story of the Iroquois tribe. It shows how the threshold may be crossed for the wrong reasons, yet gives the hope that it is possible to redeem such mistakes.

There was a young and beautiful girl who was very proud and refused all the suitors who approached her mother for her hand. This made her mother very cross. One day she took her daughter out of the village to collect firewood. While they were outside the boundary of the encampment, a sudden deep darkness descended. The mother encouraged her daughter to help her build a shelter, for it was too dark to return to the village and she knew they would have to stay the night. After supper the mother fell asleep and, when the girl looked up, she saw a magnificent young brave standing before her with a wampum bead belt and an amazing black feather headdress. He told her that he had come to marry her and would wait for her reply. The next day the girl woke her mother and told her about the handsome brave. The mother was delighted (and probably somewhat relieved) and gave her permission to continue with the courtship, so when the brave returned he took the young woman off to his camp. Having refused the call to marriage by the young men of her village, she was now on an adventure of her own — unprotected. For whereas, within the confines of the community, her mother could be her 'guardian angel', once outside those boundaries, she had no power.

The brave spent two days and two nights together with her in his wigwam, then told her he was going away to hunt. After the tent flap closed she heard a strange swishing noise yet, although curious, she carried on with her chores. In the evening she heard the strange swishing noise again and when the flap opened in slid a huge snake. The snake put his head on the amazed girl's lap and said, 'Search my head for lice, will you?' and she did. (Well you would, wouldn't you!). After she'd dealt with all sorts of unpleasant stuff on the snake's head, he slid out of the wigwam. Almost immediately the flap opened and in came the handsome brave.

'Were you afraid of me when I appeared like that just now?' he asked her and she replied, 'No.'

The next day the girl went to gather wood and saw seven serpents basking on seven rocks. She began to feel very strange and somewhat discouraged. (This always happens when you're on the wrong adventure. It's a time when decisions have to be made.) That evening the serpent slid into her wigwam again and, on its departure, in came the young brave.

On the third day, when he had gone hunting, the girl decided she would try to escape. She ran to the woods and was standing there, working out which way to go, when she heard the voice of an old man saying, 'Young lady, you are in trouble.' She stopped still and listened. The voice continued, 'The man you've married is one of seven brothers who are all great magicians. Like all such, their hearts are not in their bodies so they cannot die. You must return to the wigwam and find a bag hidden under the bed in which you will find seven hearts.'

She returned to the wigwam, quickly found the bag and ran. Suddenly she heard a voice behind her shouting 'Stop! Stop! You can never escape.' It was her husband, but she kept running and running until she was ready to faint. Then she heard the old man's voice again, saying, 'Don't worry, I'll help you,' and found herself being pulled out from under water. (This is a sort of baptism, symbolic of dying in one life and rising to live in another). When she opened her eyes, she saw that she was among seven old men who all looked alike. The story continues to tell how she was helped by them to overcome the negative magic that nearly enslaved her and to return to her mother and her tribe.

Here's how I expressed my feelings about crossing the border at the beginning of a period of great change in my life:

Boundaries

There are no boundaries
beyond the boundary.
Nothing to keep me in, them out.
Nothing to tell me where I am
in relation to everything else.
No sign saying 'You are here'.

This is a no-man's-land
of non-existence,
a place of becoming, not being.
So it is easy
to take refuge in the past,
to stay stuck in what has been,
even though it isn't any more.
So many Lilliputian cords
tie me down.
But to exist
I must break free,
cross the boundary
and plunge
into the vivacious, swelling future.

The successful withdrawal is one where the personal call is received in such a way that it is not deflected by pride, fear, desire or imagination. However, it is very easy, through lack of self-awareness, to be beguiled by a call which appeals to the wrong aspects of the psyche—desire, conceit or pride—the ego-self. Easy, too, to rationalise a call which is challenging you to break free from your past. Only the 'True Self' can respond, for only the 'True Self' will hear fully, and yet the call continues to sound, even for those who are deaf to it.

The Journey:
Once the first threshold has been crossed, the story of the mythical hero's journey is filled with encounters with forces aimed at deflecting the traveller from his or her journey. But there are also many encounters with helpers who provide all manner of magical devices to assist. The negatives may be found in the clashing rocks of the story of Jason, the hydra and the sirens in the story of Ulysses in *The Odyssey* and the distraction of Sir Lancelot by Guinevere. Consider Jonah's escape on a boat, before being swallowed by the whale, in order to get him back on track and the temptations of Jesus in the wilderness before his ministry began. The positives are found in Medea's help for Jason, Ariadne's provision of thread for Theseus, Athene's support of Ulysses and the angels opening the prison doors to the Apostle Peter.

None of these interventions are in any way under the control of the hero. Some of them succeed, some fail. The hero's rôle is to recognise help when it appears and to trust it, no matter in what guise it appears. There is one popular mythic theme in which the hero has overcome his revulsion and goes to bed with an ugly and smelly old woman. When he wakes up, he discovers she has turned into a beautiful princess. The hero must recognise when he or she is being called to dig deep and do things that are naturally revolting, and when to resist the ugliness. He or she must also discern those situations, which though attractive, must be resisted at all cost. like the sound of the sirens to Ulysses. He ended by stopping his sailors' ears and tying himself to the mast. Campbell sums this up in 'The Hero with a Thousand Faces':

> *'. . . when a heart insists on its destiny, resisting the general blandishment, then the agony is great; so too the danger. Forces,*

however, will have been set in motion beyond the reckoning of the senses. Sequences of events from the corners of the world will gradually draw together and miracles of coincidence bring the inevitable to pass.'[27]

This is something we can all see at work in our lives in retrospect. It is what Jung calls 'synchronicity', several coincidental events each leading to a specific outcome, which brings 'the inevitable to pass'. On a more practical note Ò Murchù says:

'Either through one's own initiative, or more commonly under the instigation of peers or friends, an earthing stage may follow. The spiritual seeker decides to join a meditation group, participate in a justice project, do voluntary work in a charitable organisation, have a chat with a priest or vicar, engage in a formal workshop. This can be a precarious and risky process — 'groping in the dark' — because many people who belong to religious institutions have neither the intuitive, listening or discerning skills to appreciate and understand what is happening. The perennial temptation will be to offer answers which were designed for questions belonging to another reality, namely the realm of formal religious belief.

What is most bewildering for the contemporary spiritual seeker is the cultural vacuum that often leaves spiritual explorers feeling misunderstood, disillusioned and vulnerable. It is all too easy to fall into the temptation of following the clear-cut answers offered by so many contemporary sects and cults. To provide alternative sacred spaces to the spiritual seekers of our time — with people trained in the appropriate skills of accompaniment and discernment — requires the primary and urgent attention of people of good will.'[28]

27 Campell, Joseph, The Hero with a Thousand Faces, Paladin
28 Reclaiming Spirituality, Diarmuid O'Murchu, Crossroads

The age-old mythical stories address fundamental needs of the human psyche for all ages. But they were never intended to be read literally. Their truths were to be obtained intuitively from understanding the meaning of the symbol for the individual at the time of its discernment.

Soon the hero settles into the journey. It seems there is no turning back now for those who have discovered their purpose and have the courage to step into the unknown. Ò Murchù continues:

> *'Depending on how the last stage is negotiated, there will tend to follow a stage of maturing depth and conviction, not based on secure answers, but on questions that continue to unravel the enfolding and unfolding mystery. This tends to be the stage of 'no going back'. The fascination has gripped the heart and soul; something deep within has changed profoundly. The person may not go to church or talk about "God", but deep within a transformative experience has taken root, colouring one's entire life-orientation and value appropriation.'*[29]

One outward sign of this experience is likely to be the changes for good that take place in your relationships. As your self-awareness grows, so your perceptions of others will change. You will become more tolerant and seek to understand rather than criticise. Certainly the myths indicate that the journey cannot be achieved without the hero having good relationships, both with the mystical powers sent to assist (via the unconscious) and the companions met on the way.

Modern myths, such as the "Lord of the Rings" or "Star Wars" may be more familiar to you. These stories were both developed from a thorough understanding of the mythical hero's journey, as transmitted through all cultures at all times in history. You can tell from these stories how important the relationships between friends and colleagues become, for instance, in getting Frodo to his destination and freeing the Galaxy from the evil of the Empire. We observe from these fantastical tales truths

29 Reclaiming Spirituality, Diarmuid O'Murchu, Crossroads

which can be applied directly to our own down-to-earth experience. Our helpers, like those in the ancient myths, may not always be totally willing or even particularly competent, but there seems to be an unseen force at work influencing events through them, if not directing them, in a purposeful way.

Obtaining the Boon:

What is the boon? It will usually be found within you as the result of experiencing a fully-integrated, congruent personality. However, the boon will be expressed differently in each person, for it will be expressed according to the talents and yearnings of the individual, not as something separate from him or her. Though the symbolic boon of the stories may have many connotations and interpretations, when applied to the individual, it simply represents that which is precious and unique in the hero. The boon may be the discovery of your own core purpose, or perhaps how that core purpose may be implemented for the benefit of others. At its simplest, it will be revealed in the deep life-transforming spiritual experience that will change for the better your relationship to all people and all things. At its most complex, perhaps a rôle of leadership which transforms a whole society.

Whether it's a matter of Prometheus returning with fire or my wife and I finding a new sense of personal harmony, the boon is for the benefit of the community, not just for the hero. The fire in the heart of me and my wife will surely spread to family, friends and colleagues. It can do no other. And no one will need to publicize that my wife and I have made a break-through. The experience of spiritual consciousness is like a fragrance which needs no one to bring attention to it.

Paradoxically, the boon is not always obtained by doing something. Sometimes what you are called to do is nothing at all. In this situation the boon is obtained by opening up rather than revving up. The call can be a call to practise stillness and silence, so that one obtains the boon of integration. As the Maitri Upanishad says:

> *'A quietness of mind overcomes good and evil works, and in quietness the soul is ONE: then one feels the joy of Eternity.'*

Joseph Campbell provides a very practical recommendation for achieving that quietness of soul in The Power of Myth:

> *'You must have a room, or a certain hour a day, where you don't know what was in the newspapers that morning, you don't know who your friends are, you don't know what you owe anybody, you don't know what anybody owes to you. This is a place where you can simply experience or bring forth what you are and what you might be. This is the place of creative incubation. At first you may find that nothing happens there. But if you have a sacred place and use it, something eventually will happen...'*

I have my own little epithet in this connection: *'If you can be open enough and still enough and silent enough for long enough, something wonderful happens.'*

In this situation the 'boon' is born into time. You just sit quietly bringing forth what you are. As Campbell says, you may not experience anything much at this time, but once you return to the busyness of the world, you will discover that you are taking something new with you. Something which enables you to operate from a place of peace. You'll find that you don't react so easily to the provocations you encounter or become so readily frustrated by things that get in the way of your doing what you want to do.

I met a man who had been a long time colleague some years before. We hadn't seen each other for several years, so we went for coffee to catch up. I discovered that he'd separated from his wife and so had I. He said he'd got into Eastern mysticism and, before I could express where I was spiritually, he asked 'Do you meditate?' I said that I did. He said that he could tell. There was something about me that was different from the old days. I hadn't realised it was so obvious.

That 'something' which was different may simply have been that I was more relaxed, but I knew that within me there was a lot more to it than that. Having moved from my previous position of Christian certainty, I now knew that I could not 'know', but neither could I have felt more secure. You cannot proclaim this, you can only experience it. Of those who have that experience Jesus said, 'By their fruit you shall know them.' It is therefore the expression of gracious behaviour that reveals the presence of inner peace. To the hero the boon is one thing, to those for whom it is obtained, quite another. To the hero it has to do with self-awareness and an understanding of one's core purpose. To the recipients, the boon is the action that results as the fruit of whatever has happened in the inner life of the hero.

The Return:

Richard Rohr says that the spiritual life seems to be a matter of going out and coming back; about being lost and being found. The parable of the lost coin, the lost sheep and the prodigal son all demonstrate this. This going out and coming back seems to take place on both the macro and micro level. In the Bible the macro level is in leaving the Garden of Eden and returning to Paradise with Christ. On the individual macro level the journey begins at youth and proceeds through what Shakespeare described as the 'seven ages of man'. On the micro level there are many comings and goings in life. I experience them all the time and am learning to recognise the pattern. The Tao Te Ching, resonating with Ecclesiastes, expresses it like this:

There is a time for being ahead,
a time for being behind;
a time for being in motion,
a time for being at rest;
a time for being vigorous,
a time for being exhausted;

a time for being safe,
a time for being in danger. [30]

For myself there are times of spiritual aridity and times when I feel in the flow of things. I realise that neither the aridity nor the flow will continue indefinitely. More importantly, I recognise that how I feel is how I feel, not how I am. It would be a strange and rather boring life that has no ups and downs. In any case, as someone once said to me, 'It's our imperfection that makes us human.' How can I bring the boon of peace, love and joy to others, if I do not share their experience of life?

I was once in conversation with someone who began to express deep concerns he had over issues that I had had to wrestle with years before. I recognised exactly what he was going through and was able to empathise with him and, I hope, help him to understand his situation a little better. How glad I was to have had that spiritual and intellectual wrestling match those many years before.

The boon doesn't have to be something as fabulous and rare as a Golden Fleece. It can simply be a gift for compassionate listening, the ability to make things or to bring joy and understanding through art. It may well be that no one knows you have a 'boon' but quietly and effectively over many years changes take place in the hearts and minds of those you know and love that have been enabled by your presence.

30 Tao Teh Ching 29, Stephen Mitchell.

Chapter Ten

A New Spirituality: Identifying the Ego's false self

When I refer to a 'new spirituality', I mean an experience that's new to me. Other people may well find aspects of what follows to be familiar. Although my current spiritual experience has been considerably enriched by my Christian background, it's also been enriched by the teaching of other religions and some teaching from outside conventional religion altogether. I have come to understand that religion is only a framework in which spirituality may or may not be experienced. It is essential never to get the experience confused with the framework. The whole objective of the framework is to enable adherents to transcend it. A ladder isn't something to climb for the sake of climbing. It's to reach somewhere higher. But transcending doesn't mean that you have to part from the religious body that nurtured you, as I did. I know of many people who have transcended their religion, yet are a still a positive influence within the established church. On the other hand I have met people whose former fellow-believers have turned against them and shown them the door. Each person's situation is what can be enabled in the circumstances.

***

In the first five chapters of this book I introduced you to my ego's 'false self'. Late in life I was able to recognise that my ego, rather than my 'True Self', has energised much of my behaviour, religious as well as secular. Reaching this insight meant that I had to be brutally honest with myself without descending into self-condemnation, as I would have done as a fundamentalist Christian.

The idea of there being two persons within one body, 'me and my shadow', in the words of the old song, or me and my alter-ego, is a common theme in literature. We often speak of 'being in two minds' about something. Goethe's Faust says: *'Two souls within my breast I find and each contends for mastery there.'*

One of these souls is evident even at birth. All of my babies had different ways of expressing themselves to the world and this is what Jung identified as the 'persona'. Our personas arise at the outset from genetically inherited traits and predispositions which are hard-wired and about which we can probably do little. Around this core of personality, it seems to me, we develop other traits and proclivities from our experience of life, particularly from our feelings about those experiences. These feelings may be genuine responses or may be culturally-induced prejudices. Had I been adopted and brought up in a different country by different parents, although my core genetic self would be the same, I would have developed a quite different sense of self-identity, because I would have a quite different set of life experiences. Even having remained with my birth parents, my sense of self-identify has changed several times over the years, which is further evidence that it is a false self.

Yet within each of us, there is another self, a watching Self, which is constant and consistent. This Self has not constructed a self-identity out of our experiences of life —it just is. It is the Self I encountered when, as a nine year old, I lay worrying about what my headmaster might inflict on me, until I realised there was part of me he could never reach. It is the unassailable self.

The Mundaka Upanishad has a lovely image of the relationship between the Self and the false self.

'Like two golden birds perched in the selfsame tree,
Intimate friends, the ego and the Self
Dwell in the same body. The former eats
The sweet and sour fruit of the tree of life
While the latter looks on in detachment.'[31]

It's important to note that these 'two birds' are *intimate friends*, not enemies, as Goethe would have it. It's also important to remember that the false self isn't the bad self, it's just not the True Self. The True Self loves

31 Mundaka Upanishad Part III [1] verse 1. Trans Eknath Easwaran, Arkana

the false self and, as spiritual maturity takes place, the false self grows to love and respect the True Self. If this were not so, I would never be free of the tug of fear and desire; I would always be doing, as Paul put it, 'those things I would not' and 'not doing those things I would'. It is the uniting of these two 'birds', the making whole, that is the fundamental meaning of the Biblical term 'salvation', the oneness of which the Jesus of the Gospel of John and the writers of the Upanishads speak. It is what spirituality, in the broadest meaning of the term, is all about and the purpose of all religion.

The Svetasvatara Upanishad says the active bird '. . . is the human soul who, resting on that tree, though active, feels sad in his unwisdom.' [32] This is the state we all experience from time to time, and to varying degrees. As Henry Thoreau observed, 'The mass of men live lives of quiet desperation,' and this was certainly my own state for a good part of my life. But rarely is an individual in that state all the time. Sometimes we don't experience sadness at all, because we're distracted by our current activities. But for most of us, 'quiet desperation' is lurking not far away.

Understanding my human nature

The metaphor of the false self and True Self is a useful way to explain what I experienced as a child and later, more rationally, as an adult. The false self arises, not only out of my experiences of life but out of my inbuilt biology and psychology. Let me try to explain.

Within my own lifetime scientists have gained a considerable amount of knowledge about the brain. As they've done so, a scene of unimaginable complexity has emerged—about as complex as the entire galaxy. Within the last decade or so it has been realised that we actually have at least five neural systems, each one evolved, it seems, to give us increasingly fine control over our behaviour.

Early in neural research it became clear that we have an upper brain and a lower brain, the lower divided into two parts, the upper, arguably,

32 Svetasvatara Upanishad IV, Translated by Juan Mascaro, Penguin Books

divided into three. Most recently it has been found that there is a neural network in the heart, so it might be said that we have six neural systems.

The most primitive part of the lower brain is called the 'reptilian brain'. It's our 'crocodile' within. This was the first neural network to evolve in our species, long before we were human. Its purpose is to respond to movement and shape, according to what has become known as 'the four Fs': fight, flee, feed and—well—make love. These are reflex actions determined on primarily whether the brain perceives a threat, a meal or a mate.

Jung described a function of the mind which he called 'sensation' and said this function simply tells us something is there. I suggest that this seems to fit with the function of the reptilian brain. Its bottom line is to focus on what it senses and to respond instinctively, rather than rationally. People controlled primarily by the primitive instincts of the lower brain are capable of deeply selfish acts, from theft or cruelty to major atrocities. Yet we all experience instinctive reactions. If someone gets angry with me, my most immediate reaction is to feel angry too.

Later, to supplement the reptilian brain, the mammalian brain evolved but nature doesn't always shed earlier developments. The functions of the 'Mark I' reptilian brain were kept and 'Mark II' became a kind of supercharged auxiliary. The mammalian brain is more sophisticated than the reptilian. In crude terms it can assess situations, not merely by shapes and movements, but by how it feels about those shapes and movements. Jung described a part of the mind he called 'feelings' which, he said, are not so much about emotion, but about evaluation and judgement of the degree of friendliness, threat or edibility. A crocodile may not be able to help itself from snapping at a passer-by, because it has to respond to its instinct. A primitive mammal may choose to ignore the instinct trigger altogether. For instance, today a gazelle may ignore a passing lion because it perceives that the lion's not hungry. But yesterday the lion was hunting and the gazelle ran like hell.

Later still, 'Mark III', the cerebral cortex evolved. This gave us highly sophisticated spatial, verbal, memory, creative, and logic faculties.

It was like upgrading a 286 MSDOS computer to one with a dual core Pentium chipset. But however powerful our cerebral cortex may be, we still experience the instinctive triggers from the lower, mammalian and reptilian brains. (Think of it as being like the old MSDOS operating system which runs silently underneath Windows.) With the new brain we're equipped to actually *choose* how to respond to those instinctive triggers, using a wide range of techniques both learned and created on the spot. Sadly we often don't choose to use them, but react automatically. This, surely, is the cause of much mayhem in human societies worldwide.

To some extent, what enables our choices of action is yet another brain evolution, the frontal lobes. This area, seated at the front of the brain immediately behind the forehead, appears to govern, among other things, the way we choose to express ourselves and socialise with others. It seems to co-ordinate aspects of instinct and thinking arising in other parts of the brain. It is interesting to note that ancient mystics have often associated special faculties with a 'third eye' located in the centre of the forehead. The mystical Kundalini snake is depicted as emerging from the forehead or the top of the head in Indian pictures and statues, and was part of the headdress of pharaohs. Psychiatrists have also discovered that some psychopaths have defects in their frontal lobes which inhibit their ability to empathise with other people. This can arise from genetic inheritance or by the conditions that existed when the brain was being formed during early babyhood.

The recent discoveries of Dr. J. Andrew Armour show that the heart has a source of intelligence so powerful he calls it the 'heart brain'.[33] A whole new medical profession, cardio-neurology, has opened up as a result. Research is beginning to reveal that the heart may have an even greater rôle in coordinating brain activities than has the cerebral cortex. So maybe Pascal was more right than he could possibly know when he said, *'The heart has its reasons which reason knows nothing of'*.

---

33 The Coherent Heart, R. McCraty, Ph.D., M. Atkinson, D. Tomasino, B.A., R. Trevor Bradley, Ph.D. INTEGRAL REVIEW December 2009 Vol. 5, No. 2

The main problem, as I see it, is that, although we have the immense power of the upper brain at our disposal, we haven't yet learned to manage adequately the strong instinctive signals coming from the lower brain. This is why, no matter how well educated and intellectually sophisticated we may be, we can still be drawn into taking inappropriate action provoked by fear and desire. Indeed, our animal nature, which provokes fear and desire, is a repeating theme in mythological images, even from the earliest days of our cultural beginnings. Depicted as the Green Man found on carvings in British churches, it can also be found in the images of half-goat, half-human Pan and Satan, or the elephant-headed god, Ganesh. Gebser points out that among the earliest examples of art are images of the human figure entangled by vegetation.[34] Over thousands of years art evolved to show the human figure becoming gradually less entangled. By the 14th century human figures began to appear in full perspective, standing in relief against a natural background. But although our consciousness seems to be on an upwar,d evolutionary trajectory, we clearly have a long way to go as a species, before we're free of the pressures arising from our basic reptilian and mammalian instincts.

Over the last few centuries a condition emerged that has created much of the chaos we experience in contemporary society. Arising from over-arousing the instinctive urges of our primitive brain, Deirdre Barrett calls it 'supernormal stimuli'.[35] One aspect of this phenomenon, which illustrates the condition well, comes from our bodies having evolved to want fat and sweet food. In our primitive state, this was not a problem because, having gorged ourselves on a catch or eaten the contents of a hive, we might not eat properly again for days or weeks. Now, we can take these same primitive instincts to the Burger Bar day after day and have a half-pounder with cheese and double fries, followed by dessert topped with extra cream. Then we can waddle back to the sofa to watch sit-coms and wash it all down with cola. Marketing experts use 'super-normal stimuli' to appeal to

---

34 The Ever Present Origin, Jean Gebser, Ohio University Press.

35 Supernormal Stimuli, Deirdre Barrett, W.W. Norton, NY 2009, IBSN 978-0393068481

our basic instincts with ever bigger, better, more colourful or sexier images.

When sugar and tobacco became popular in the 17th century, they changed our dietary and social habits, as well as our general health. In those days the cost of such luxuries put them out of the reach of the masses. It was mainly the rich who suffered from badly rotting teeth. This was perhaps the first incidence of exposure to 'super-normal stimuli'. Now our brains are assailed from morning to night with super-normal stimuli pedalling music, drugs, alcohol, pornography, computer games, mobile phones, fairground rides, television shows, shopping, fast food, fast cars and hundreds of other sources of ego-elevation. These are all bait to the voracious appetites of the lower brain and, for many of us, the effects are supercharged by the appeal to the ego's 'false self'— it makes us feel good or look good and drives us into a feeding frenzy.

The false self wants, either to stand out from the crowd in a positive way, one which attracts admiration and status, or to merge with the crowd so that feels protected and secure. To achieve this it will choose non-conformity or conformity, whichever is most acceptable to its social group and to its own comfort. It doesn't care about the context. For the false self, conformity with a religious body is just as effective a palliative as conformity in a night club. Contrariness about politics can be just as ego-elevating as contrariness about religion or atheism. 'Whatever turns you on!'

Though we can't locate our ego, there's no denying we all experience it and recognise it in others. There may be times when the primitive urge is too strong for us to resist and so we use our cerebral logic faculty to rationalise an excuse for giving in. I might rationalise that since I gave in on my diet this morning, I might as well give in this afternoon and start dieting tomorrow. Yet, in other circumstances, I could use that same logic faculty to rationalise a different stance and resist the temptation. The big problem in all this is not so much our giving in or resisting, or even having the desires themselves, it is in thinking that the feelings provoked by the desires are who we are: 'I'm happy.' 'I'm sad.' 'I'm lonely.' 'I'm the life and soul of the party.' 'I'm depressed.' The Mundaka Upanishad goes on to say this:

'As long as we think we are the ego,
We feel attached and fall into sorrow.'

The ego's 'false self' begins to develop very early in life. As I've shown, mine did so in response to my experiences of other people—parents, sister, grandparents, aunts, uncles, teachers, friends and enemies, as well as to my environment. It has grown largely from memories of experiences and, in particular, memories of feelings I had during those experiences: how I felt about my early head teacher's put-downs, my successes and failures in subsequent schools, the jobs I had and the girls I fell in and out of love with.

Feelings are largely an activity of the lower, mammalian and reptilian brain complex, which is known as the limbic system. Ego-experiences often have little or nothing to do with reality. They are largely my left brain's interpretation of my lower brain's instinctive responses, generated, at least in part, by an element of the limbic system called the hippocampus. Those who suffer damage to the hippocampus lose some of their cognitive faculties, showing that the faculties of instinct and recognition are closely linked. The upper brain tries to find a reason for arousal in the hippocampus and, if none is obvious, it makes one up—in other words, rationalises one. Putting it crudely: if another child treated me spitefully and called me by a rude name, my instinctive reaction would be fight or flight. If it's flight, I might run away or, if that's not possible, bury my head in my hands and cry, my brain rationalising that I must be weak and cowardly because that's how I feel. If the reaction is fight, then I'd wade in with my fists and, if I won, I'd feel brave and strong, and my brain would rationalise that is what I am.

Thomas Harris described this in terms of feeling OK or not OK Although published a good few years ago, Harris's model is as relevant today as it has always been. It illustrates the operation of the 'false self' in me very well. He suggests four conditions of thinking: 'I'm OK, you're OK', 'I'm not OK, you're OK', I'm OK, you're not OK and 'I'm not OK, you're not OK'

Most of us find ourselves experiencing the 'You're OK, I'm not OK.' syndrome from time to time. It arises when we are among people we don't know or among people we consider to be superior to ourselves. Starting a new job, for instance, where everyone knows what's what and you know nothing. Perhaps in a situation where we feel out of our depth: a young parent attending the PTA for the first time for instance. It can even be observed among friends, when the hostess apologizes that the meal wasn't quite as it should have been. Perhaps also when she responds to a compliment on her appearance, by replying that her outfit isn't new. This is likely to be a response of the 'false self' and may have been induced by overbearing parents telling her how to behave in public. Such behaviour can be brought about by dominating teachers or the neighbourhood bully. At its most psychotic, the 'I'm not OK' syndrome may lead to depression, substance or alcohol abuse, or over-eating. Fortunately most of us won't reach that stage.

However, some people over-compensate for this underlying sense of inferiority. They take up an attitude of 'I'm OK, you're not OK.' They project their bad feelings on to others and this is the approach of many bullies. Their 'false selves' assume everyone else is inferior, for it may then be reasonable to assume they are superior. It may also be the position of the dominating teacher who embarked on a career in education to overcome his feelings of inferiority. He makes up for not feeling OK by making his students feel inferior. His own feelings of inadequacy can be easily provoked, so any challenge to his authority will be met by reptilian violence. Most usually this is verbal, but only because actual physical violence is no longer legal. However, in recent years, there have been numerous cases where a teacher has suddenly become violent, being unable to repress his feelings of hurt any longer.

A third state described by Harris is 'I'm not OK, you're not OK'. In a way, this describes my experience of my junior school headmaster.

Fortunately this didn't develop into an acute condition. But when it does, the 'I'm not OK, you're not OK' state can lead to isolation and chronic depression. It can also result in violent behaviour such as that which arises among young people caught up with inner city gangs. Their home lives have induced a feeling of being unloved and they feel threatened by other people. They don't feel good about themselves and they've no reason to feel good about others. To try to make themselves feel good, they do what they can to make others feel bad.

The best state, which is the title of Harris's book, is 'I'm OK. you're OK'. This is when I feel good about myself and good about other people too. I live securely with Elizabeth in a pleasant location, surrounded by lovely friends, and my children are all happily married. So I feel OK—most of the time. It is the best state most people achieve and yet we cannot regard it as permanent, for it is externally stimulated. It's all too easy for something to arise which disrupts life's tranquillity. Too quickly I can be plunged back into the false self's 'I'm not OK' state. An unexpected bill, a family upset or someone getting angry with me can provoke feelings of serious discomfort.

We are all likely to experience these four mental states at different times and our memories colour the good and bad feelings we get with justification or excuse. But memories aren't real. The events they represent are long gone, yet the feelings are part of a personal repertoire that can easily be provoked into a performance. I've been dragging many of them through my life as if they still existed, and they've often adversely affected my responses to current events. Like Eckhart's 'hides' my memories and feelings have covered up my True Self and allowed the ego's 'false self', to colour the way I respond to people and situations every day. For many years I thought I *was* my 'false self' and that's why I kept, as the Mundaka puts it, *falling into sorrow.* But I am not my thoughts. I am not my feelings. I am not my memories, I am not my imagination. I AM.

Fear and Desire

We keep *falling into sorrow* because the ego responds strongly to two psychic forces—and by 'psychic 'I don't mean paranormal or occult, I simply mean 'of the mind.' They are fear and desire. Each of these forces has two aspects: functional and dysfunctional. The functional aspect is important to our survival. If I don't learn to be afraid of hungry lions or burning forests, I won't last long. If I don't know how to desire good, my life will be mediocre, to say the least. Problems arise when desire and fear become dysfunctional. This may be when I fear imaginary situations or recall fear from the past. It may occur when I fear loss of face, or desire unnecessary or illicit things for the sake of status or pleasure. On such occasions my body responds to my mind's feeling 'not OK' by generating biochemicals, such as cortisol or adrenalin. In my primitive state I would have burned these off by rushing around, yelling with joy or thumping my chest and roaring threats. (I admit I've been known to get a bit like that in the past). But if I did that in polite, modern company, I would lose face and that's not OK either, so the biochemicals arise but don't get burned off and my body suffers from their poison, making me feel worse.

The ego's primary objective is to make me feel OK, and there's nothing wrong with that. But there's a mechanism of the lower brain, the amygdala, which responds to anomalies out of pure instinct. The amygdala's job is to ready the body for action but, again, it can't tell from where the stimulus is coming: the lower brain's perception of a threat or the upper brain's imagined or remembered threat. It will therefore ready the body for action whether the threat is coming from outside, perceived through the senses, or from inside, perceived from memory or imagination.

It will also respond to a real opportunity for food or sex - or an imaginary one in the same way. This is why the very thought of strawberries and cream could make my great-uncle dribble, and the thought of school could make me feel sick. Thus the ego can stimulate a physical response from what is only imagination. Such a response makes the ego feel real. It can fool itself into thinking it has status through owning things or through exhibiting superior skills. It reasons: 'I am who I am because I'm valued or feared by others.' If I think I look good and I feel good, then all is well. A shower and a nicely pressed outfit will do that. But if something goes wrong, if I'm held up on a journey, or someone is rude to me, or if I feel unwell, the ego feels threatened and fear sets in. This, Richard Rohr says, is the fear of death that Paul speaks of; not physical death, but death of the ego, or perhaps more accurately, the ego's 'false self'. When the only self we know is the false-self, its extinction is terrifying.

The ego-centred life is therefore a constant tussle between desire and fear. Desire for things and fear I won't get them. Desire for status and fear of losing it. Desire to be respected for who I think I am and fear that the ego's false sense of self will be exposed. Our days are full of little sufferings, yet we've become highly adept at ignoring them, always hoping for something better just around the corner.

A Buddhist Perspective

This ego condition was graphically illustrated for me when I visited the Todai-ji Buddhist temple at Nara, the ancient capital of Japan. In the entrance gate of the temple are two huge statues each of which has a human body and a monstrous dragon-like head. The one on the left looks alarmed and is holding its left hand out like a police officer holding up traffic. It represents fear. The one on the right is similar but its mouth is open and its right hand is grasping. It represents desire. Devotees and visitors have to pass between these two 'guardians of the way' to get into the outer court of the temple. I noticed that to do so we had to climb several steps. This meant paying attention. We had to cross mindfully over the threshold between the two monsters of fear and desire.

We then walked through a courtyard—a wide space, perhaps representing freedom and peace, in which to contemplate the symbolic act we had just performed. Then, having carried out the necessary washing of hands, symbolically cleansing ourselves of thoughts that inhibit our spiritual lives, we went into the temple where there were two imposing statues of the Buddha. One had its right hand raised, using the gesture known in India as the Gyan Mudra, which represents the spiritual home. The gesture contrasted with the right-handed grasp of the monster of desire at the gate. It's meaning for me was that, when I am centred in my spiritual home, dysfunctional desire has no place in me. The other statue has its left hand held up in blessing; a perfect counterpoint to the monster of fear we had passed to enter the temple. When I am centred in my spiritual home, without dysfunctional desire, fear can have no hold over me.

All Change

Once I had recognised the implication of the two birds in the tree, the (True) Self and the (false) self, and had understood the nature of the false self, nothing could remain the same. Many of life's distractions, which had dogged my path as a fundamentalist Christian, fell away. If dysfunctional fear comes knocking on my door, I can recognise it for what it is and, in doing so, it usually slinks off into the night. If dysfunctional desire begins to beguile me, I can also recognise it and name it, putting it to flight. This doesn't make me a saint, for this is an ongoing process. But most of the time my 'two souls' do not 'contend for mastery', they live in the peace, love and joy of being united.

Most importantly of all, I recognise I am not my 'false self'. I am not the 'OK' or 'Not OK' feelings I experience from time to time; these are feelings, that's all. I am not my fears or desires. They are simply things I experience. Only after this recognition could I enter more fully into an experience of the mysterious 'True Self'; the bird which observes without comment.

Finally, here's a little check list you might like to use to help identify some of the subtle activities of the false self. Remember, there's nothing intrinsically wrong with most of these behaviours; they simply betray that we are not fully at rest in the presence of the True Self.

- Getting impatient—pacing about when I'm waiting for a bus or waiting for someone who's still getting ready to go out.
- Retaliating with an unkind remark when someone upsets me.

- Being envious when someone else has something I'd like to have—a better car, a smarter outfit, a better holiday.
- Embellishing stories about me in order to impress.
- Feeling a smirk appear on my face when someone praises me. Hoping to be noticed.
- Getting upset when, having given way to someone on the road, they don't acknowledge my good deed.
- Feeling left out when I'm in a group and no one's talking to me or about me. Feeling hurt because I wasn't invited.
- Feeling hurt when I think I'm being criticized—or even when I really am being criticized.
- Being rude to telesales people who call at an inappropriate moment. Being rude to someone simply because I'm in a bad mood.
- Taking the last chocolate. Getting my way—albeit surreptitiously. Not being mindful of the needs of others.
- Getting angry when things don't go my way or something hinders my progress. Anger is frustration projected outwardly, either at an object or a person. Typical responses may be to kick it or swear at it.
- Bearing a grudge. Waiting for an apology before I speak to someone.
- Indulging in activities that appeal to my baser side. Ignoring my conscience.
- Failing to protect others by appropriate intervention—passing by on the other side.
- Being untrusting, cynical or contrary. Especially if the motive is to make myself look superior.
- Falling into despair or giving up too easily.

You might like to compare the items in this list with the character of love in 1 Corinthians 13:4-8 mentioned earlier:

Love is patient, love is kind.

It does not envy, it does not boast,
It is not proud
It is not rude
It is not self-seeking

It is not easily angered
And it keeps no record of wrong.

Love does not delight in evil
But rejoices with the truth.

It always protects,
Always trusts,
Always hopes,
Always perseveres.
Love never fails.

Chapter Eleven

A New Spirituality: Recognising my True Self

To discover, or unmask, the 'false self' is important, but transformation, the great *metanoia*, can only takes place when we discover the 'True Self'. This, I found, I could realise most fully only by taking time to be still and silent. As a result my awareness expanded and I could become more fully conscious of the 'True Self'. As this happened, so I also became more aware of others. This, I discovered, is an inevitable result of such an awakening.

To some extent self and other awareness can simply be the outcome of personal development, or improved emotional intelligence. I had been deeply involved in personal development work throughout my years as a careers adviser and trainer, and latterly had been heavily involved in helping people to develop their practical emotional-intelligence skills. But if I hadn't gone further than this personally, I would have remained a prisoner of the ego's 'false self'. Not that I am claiming to be totally free of ego, but there are states beyond 'personal development' which are deeper, richer, more profound and more satisfying than anything that can be achieved by merely improving the persona or reconciling it with the shadow self.

The experience of the 'True Self', I found, is a feature that runs like a golden thread through most of the world's religions, even though their understanding of the divine and the terminology they use is so diverse. For instance, Paul was a committed monotheist, and regarded "God" as a separate entity. The writers of the Upanishads were pantheists. They believed "God" is everything and everything is "God". The Greeks and Romans were polytheists and had a whole pantheon of gods. Buddhists and Taoists are non-theists who don't have words to describe thoughts about such a mystery as "God".

Yet, notwithstanding all these different perceptions of the divine, each religion teaches a core of divinity that exists in everyone. In Christian terms it is expressed as 'Christ within'. It is also the Tao of the Taoists, the

Ruah, or Spirit, of the Torah and the Atman or Self of the Upanishads. In Greece, Stoic philosophers spoke of the 'Logos', which was considered to be the divine influence in the universe and the individual. Romans thought of the 'Genius', which was a spark of divinity individual to each person. The Lurianic Kaballah, holy book of some Jewish mystics, also speaks of a spark of divinity which exists in each person coming into the world.

Some theologians try to reconcile the differences between pantheism, polytheism, non-theism and monotheism. They speak of 'panentheism'; that is "God" *in* all things. Some Christians think panentheism may be implied in Jesus' statement in the Gospel of John, '*I and the Father are.*' I had always interpreted this 'oneness' to be about the exclusive relationship between Jesus and his heavenly Father. However, in his prayer at the end of John, Jesus asked *'that they may be one as we are one'*. This infers he did not consider the 'oneness' to be exclusively his. It is something we all have—even me.

This is not the kind of relationship with the divine I had ever considered as a fundamentalist Christian. I had thought of "God" as a supreme overlord and me as one of His many minions—and a pretty insignificant one at that. I later discovered this idea of oneness with "God" is present in the Bible, but my literalist doctrines had made me blind to them. Literalist theology had driven a massive chasm between me and my Christian "God", which took years to heal.

I've come to recognise that the 'false self' sees everything in terms of pairs of opposites: right and wrong, true and false, good and bad. Its instinct is to divide and separate in a judgemental way and this is probably the easiest way to recognise the 'false self'. The 'True Self' always seeks to unite—always. That doesn't mean it can't discern right from wrong, true from false or good from bad, but that it doesn't feel threatened by the opposites as the 'false self' does. It is the 'True Self' that may be said to be 'one with the father' and it is this oneness that is the unassailable foundation of real spiritual experience. Jung describes the Self as a void, a nothing—not in the sense of emptiness, but of that which cannot be known, because there is no opposite. It is a wholeness, a completeness, not a deficiency. The ego which, thinks it is a something, although it's not, cannot bear a vacuum and so is always in opposition to the True Self. The wholeness reveals the ego's deficiency. 'The light shines in darkness and the darkness comprehended it not.'

It is the experience of oneness with the True Self to which the mystics of all religions, including Christian mystics, have been referring down the centuries. For instance, John, in his first letter, says '. . .*those who live in love, live in "God"*, [36] and this is nearer to my concept of the 'True Self' than the Almighty Father figure I once thought of. In the Tao Teh Ching we read, '. . . *he who cultivates the Tao is one with the Tao.*'[37] And again, the Mundaka Upanishad says the wise '. . . *have attained the unitive state and . . . have become one with the Lord of love.*'[38] The Islamic poet, Kabir, wrote:

> *Where are you searching for me, friend?*
> *Look! Here am I right within you.*
> *Not in temple, nor in mosque,*
> *Not in Kaaba, nor Kailas,*
> *But here right within you am I.*[39]

I was astonished to find that this principle of oneness is also built into the very fabric of the universe. This is corroborated by modern scientific discovery. When I stand in the moonlight, photons from the moon enter my body and become one with the elements of my body. Of course, the same is true of sunlight. The elements of my body have 'sensitivity' to light and photons have a 'quantum stickiness' that leaves something of themselves in my body. I'm not just looking on, like seeing a picture of the moon on a screen. I'm participating in 'moonness' and it is participating in

36 1 John 3:4

37 Tao Teh Ching 23, Trans: John C.H. Wu, Shambhala

38 Mundaka Upanishad 2:1, Trans: Eknath Easwaran, The Upanishads, Arkana

39 Songs of Kabir, Translated by Rabindranath Tagore, MacMillan (1915)

me. The two of us have become one.[40] Maybe this is what Michael Dowd means when he speaks of an 'evidential understanding of reality'. It is an empirical realisation of ancient teaching about oneness.

My understanding is that my acceptance into this relationship of oneness with whatever it is we refer to as "God", is completely and utterly unconditional. It isn't something that happens to me as a result of being 'born again'. This expression only describes my becoming conscious of that unconditional and loving relationship which has *always* existed. There is nothing I could have done to create that relationship with the 'True Self' because it has *always* been the same. It is '. . . *the light that lighteneth every man that cometh into this world.'* [41] Better still, there is nothing, absolutely nothing, I can do to stop it from continuing. It is all of grace. The only thing that can come between me and an experience of the 'True Self' is my mind. Even so, my mind cannot stop the relationship, only my experience of it.

For me, the awareness of oneness was sparked in me when I was nine, but it arose in me, and is still arising, very gradually after many years of contemplation. For others it comes suddenly, like the way a skeletal drawing of a cube flips from one angle to another, if you look at it long enough. Suddenly, "God" is no longer 'out there' but 'in here'. Rather than original sin, which was a burden I carried throughout my Christian days, I began to realise that I was part of something much more wonderful—original goodness.

40 The Universe is a Green Dragon, Brian Swimme, Bear & Company, Inc.

41 John 1:9, A Catholic Interlinear New Testament Polyglot: Volume 1Veritatus Splendor Publications

Chapter Twelve

Original Goodness

If at my very core I am the Eternal Self, then rather than being intrinsically bad, as my Christianity had taught me, I must actually be intrinsically good. What a relief! My fellow Christians and I laid heavy stress on the doctrine of 'original sin', taking our authority from Paul's letters to the Romans 5: *'Therefore, just as sin entered the world through one man, and death through sin, in this way death came to all men, because all sinned.'* This appears to say that we inherited sinfulness from the fall of Adam. The flesh, we were taught, is inherently sinful, which is why Jesus had to die to pay the penalty for our sin and allay the wrath of "God". However, I eventually discovered it wasn't until the fourth century that the concept of original sin appeared in church doctrine. Augustine of Hippo developed the idea, probably taking it from Paul's statement in Romans. It was never recorded as a doctrine taught by Jesus.

Since the time of Augustine the doctrine of 'original sin' has created lots of opportunities for Christians to beat themselves up and grovel before "God". The Roman church even insists on baptising babies, especially sickly ones, so if they should die, they won't have to spend too much time in purgatory as a punishment for sin—despite the fact they don't even know the meaning of the word 'sin', let alone had a chance to actually commit any. Original sin laid a heavy burden of shame and guilt on generations of people, which we lugged around despite our gospel message of forgiveness.

Jesus said '*the kingdom is within you*' [42] and he didn't regard that oneness with the father as exclusively his. Therefore I have been 'one with the father' not simply from the date of my 'accepting Jesus as my personal saviour' or since my baptism, but always. It follows there must be another aspect of my being which transcends 'original sin'. Eknath Easwaran called this 'original goodness'. If I'd ever thought of myself as being

42 Luke 17:21 (This passage is often given the translation 'among' instead of within and that for purely theological reasons. In 14 other places *entos* is translated 'within'.)

inherently good instead of inherently bad, I think my life, especially my religious life, could have been more about peace, love and joy, and much less about guilt, fear and shame. Not that my life was without peace, love and joy. You can't have a brush with the True Self without experiencing something of its fruits, however bogged down by dogma you are. That's what grace is about, but I had struggled with Paul's words in Romans 6: 'You are not under law but under grace.' I thought this to be true, simply because the 'divinely inspired' Paul had said it, but I didn't *feel* it. What I felt was the burden of guilt from original sin which derived from my having to live in 'the flesh', which, to Paul, was the source of evil. Once I realised I was embedded in 'original goodness' because 'I and the father are one', I could find peace. I am whole because wholeness has always been an integral aspect of me. This is not dependent on my holding the correct beliefs or even doing the right things. In computer terms, 'oneness' is my default setting. This surely was the gospel of Jesus—even if it wasn't the gospel of Paul.

For me the solution was not to fight against original sin with my will, but to surrender my will to original goodness. As a Christian I had fully agreed with those who told me I couldn't do it myself, only "God" could do it, but He never did. I was always falling back into my old ways and feeling that, however hard I prayed for the strength to overcome my inherent sinfulness, "God" never gave it. This, I interpreted, was because I was unworthy.

But now I understand I was seeing the whole situation as 'in a mirror, obscurely'—and when we see in a mirror, we see things the wrong way round. I had been trying to fight myself with myself, which was like one-armed wrestling with me as the only contender! What I had to learn was what psychologist Carl Rogers called 'unconditional positive regard': firstly towards myself—and in particular towards my old enemy, my 'false self', which is a principle included in Jesus' injunction to 'love your enemy'. Then, and only then could I fulfil what spirituality is about: unconditional regard toward others.

There are distinct differences in the ways in which the 'True Self' and the 'false self' operate in the mind. The 'false self' tends to drive. There is an urgency in it, which impels me toward an object of desire or away from an object of fear. The 'True Self' is totally non-coercive. It observes with compassion. There is a tenderness about it that comforts and supports those who sense its presence. It prompts me and draws me towards what is needed but not towards self-satisfaction as an end in itself. As I become more identified with my 'True Self' so I become less identified with my 'false self'. As I become more identified with my 'True Self', so I become less conscious of my little self and *my* needs, and more conscious of others and *their* needs. Instead of being driven to react negatively with those who deal with me harshly, I am drawn to act compassionately. I seek to understand which pain is provoking their behaviour and to see in them the same 'True Self' I find in me.

Most importantly I have come to see that as I draw closer to the 'True Self', so my attitude toward my 'false self' becomes more compassionate. No longer do I regard it with fear or hatred, but acceptance. It is, after all, only that aspect of my mind which arises, at least in part, out of the instincts of the lower, primitive brain, augmented by memories of feelings and words. The instincts are largely to do with self-preservation and procreation, and these are essential functions but carry with them certain redundancies for us. I eventually saw that, although my 'false self' might be regarded as an enemy of the 'True Self', Jesus said I should love my enemies. Loving my 'false self' brought me into a new relationship with it. No longer did it 'contend for mastery' to the same degree I'd previously experienced. Those two birds, as the Upanishad says, are after all, intimate friends.

The truth of this unity is slowly expanding within me. I began to realise that I am one with that which enables the universe. I am therefore one with every *thing* in the universe. Such oneness is the foundation of Jesus' teaching and, I believe, the basis of all spiritual living. I've meditated upon this oneness for forty years and my experience of it deepens, albeit slowly. Perhaps this is why the sages speak of it as love, for a loving relationship with another person operates in the same way. It gets deeper and more profound as the years pass and one never tires of it. This sense of oneness, or 'oneing' as Julian of Norwich referred to it, leads to a deep experience of peace, which is the first fruit of the spirit.

Fruits of the Spirit

From reading a wide range of scriptures, as I have observed previously, I find that there are three primary 'fruits of the spirit': peace, love and joy, and with this Paul agrees, adding forbearance, kindness, goodness, faithfulness, gentleness and self-control [43]. On first sight the primary three appeared to be separate entities, but that's only because I experience each one differently. In all other respects I can't help thinking they are actually three facets of the same mystery, for they seem to be co-dependent. Let me explain:

Until I am at peace, I cannot fully love. Once I experience love, then the fruit of love is joy. Peace, then, is the ground out of which love grows, of which joy is the inevitable fruit. These three are not my goal but my performance indicators. I can measure my spiritual temperature by how fully I experience peace, love and joy in my life. Even during times of spiritual aridity, my longing for them encourages me to wait rather than move rashly in the wrong direction. As Rumi says, *'. . . the beloved is absence as well as this fullness.'* [44] The 'True Self' is the source of my experience of peace, love and joy, and is also the source of my longing for the experience when it is not current. But entering into an experience of the fruits of the spirit is not a matter of my achievement. Such an experience doesn't arise out of my 'fighting the good fight' and being good enough to earn the reward of "God". Rather it arises spontaneously out of the simple recognition of the work of the 'True Self' in my life. What I'm experiencing is the core of who I really am. I surrender to what's already there.

43 Galatians 5:22, 23

44 Rumi: Bridge to the soul—9, The Time of Divulging—Trans Coleman |Barks, Harper Collins

Peace

I read the words of Lao Tzu: *'The peaceful and serene is the norm of the world'* [45]. To we who are caught up in our ego-frenzy, such a statement seems ridiculous, yet my heart told me it is true. Looking back over the decades of my life, I observe that the frenzy never lasts; a storm doesn't blow all night. Lao Tzu continues: peace comes with the morning. Indeed, strikes and wars all resolve in some level of peace. Even when a lion has taken a gazelle, it's not long before the herd is quietly grazing again. The herd doesn't bring in the psychiatrists to deal with post-traumatic stress. No teams of counsellors are needed to help them get over the shock of their loss. Serenity and peace are at the core of nature. (I'm in full sympathy with those who suffer from PTS or need support from counsellors. What I'm saying here is that we humans have memories, imaginations and egos that make us far more vulnerable to stress than the rest of the natural world.)

The desire for peace by humans is endemic. Search the web and you find thousands of sites offering soft-spoken relaxation-inducing meditation CDs, literature on well-being or music designed to help you chill out. We have a radio station, Classic FM, which has hours of time devoted to the slow movements of symphonies and concertos to calm listeners down. In America, it is estimated that the meditation market (!) will reach $2 billion per annum by 2022. Such markets arise because it is widely recognised that our frenetic lifestyle is not just uncomfortable, it's bad for our health. It produces heart-attacks, strokes, skin diseases, depression and a multitude of other ailments. Despite knowing this, we're caught up in an unstoppable mad merry-go-round.

What usually passes for peace is an absence of strife, but that's only a temporary condition, not the 'peace that passes all understanding', of which Paul speaks. Temporary peace is actually only placidity, like the calm water on the surface of a lake. But once the wind comes, the lake surface is far from placid. There's nothing wrong with placidity but it doesn't last. The peace I'm referring to is like the deep water under the

45 Tao Teh Ching 45, Trans: John CH Wu, Shambhala

surface of the lake, a peace which underlies all of existence. No matter what happens on the surface, that deep peace is still there because, unlike the placid experiences induced by external factors, this peace is the permanent me. It's not something that comes and goes, as does my experience of it. It *is* the True Self, not an aspect of it. What I've had to do is learn to plunge deep into it, especially when the surface of my mind is in danger of being churned up by the gales of life. I've had to learn to reconnect with those permanent depths and recognise true peace is still there, whatever is going on up top. It is sometimes possible to find it by guided meditations or ethereal music but such inducement isn't always convenient. I needed to learn to realise it by detaching myself from the drag chains of fear and desire, and I found this was more a matter of letting go than bringing on.

The peace spoken of by Paul and said by John to be bequeathed by Jesus, is a much deeper and wider experience than can normally be found through external factors. The Greek word for peace, used in the New Testament, is *eirēnē*, and one connotation is 'being united again' [46]—a clear reference to oneness, which we will find is true of all three fruits. Chilton Pearce uses the term 'unconflicted' in relation to the thinking mind and I get the sense that when a mind is at peace, it is because it is no longer in conflict, either with itself or with anyone else—certainly not with the True Self. Peace may also be said to be the experience of being in the flow of something; knowing you are performing at the peak of your ability and even the difficult things seem easy. I guess it's epitomised in the experience of authors and poets when they're 'in the flow' and the words pour onto the page effortlessly. It may also be like the experience of athletes who, having trained to peak fitness, know they're performing at their best. Maybe like a jazz musician when he or she improvises effortlessly in collaboration with other players. In more everyday terms, it's about knowing I'm in the right place at the right time doing the right thing in the right way.

46 The Expository Dictionary of New Testament Words, W.E. Vine, Oliphant.

Love

Although love and peace are, in one sense, integral to one another, it may also be said that love grows out of a sense of peace. If I'm not at peace, it is difficult for me to love someone as fully as possible. Anyone who, like me, has lived through the stresses and strains of bringing up a family, will understand that. When I'm not experiencing peace, what Eckhart Tolle calls my pain-body is getting in the way. Instead of forgiving, I find myself criticizing, blaming and projecting my guilt on to the other. The voice of the True Self, my source of true love, is blocked out and therefore I can't love fully, but this doesn't mean love isn't still present within me.

I experience love because at the very core of my being. *I am* love—not the sloppy sentimental stuff of Hollywood movies, but the strong love which expresses itself in compassionate action. Indeed, compassion, it seems to me, is the executive arm of love. It is through compassion others experience my love. It draws them into a relationship with me for, like peace, love is a unity. Plato said, *'Love is the pursuit of the whole,'* and this, rather neatly, points us back once again to the unity of all things. For cosmologist Brian Swimme, love is the human expression of that same 'allurement' which brings hydrogen atoms together to form helium and create a sun.[47] Such allurement is expressed in the Kena Upanishad as Tadvanam, one of the names of Brahman, meaning 'the end of love longing.'

Joy

There is a vast difference between joy and happiness. 'Hap' is the old English word for luck, so happiness has to do with lucky events. Happiness comes about as a result of something external *happening* which makes me feel good. Long may such things occur. But joy can arise when nothing is happening. It can even arise when bad things are happening. With happiness, I have to take action to gain it—I have to do something, buy something, go somewhere nice, meet nice people, listen to good music or have fun dancing or drinking or even going to a church, mosque or temple.

---

47 The Universe is a Green Dragon, Brian Swimme, Bear & Company.

Without a stimulus to happiness, many of us don't know how to be happy, because happiness is only experienced as the fruit of action. But joy is the fruit of love and love is an aspect of my very being. The Taittiriya Upanishad says,

> *'And then he saw that Brahman was joy: for from joy all beings have come, by joy they all live, and unto joy they all return.'* [48]

What a wonderful thought! That we each have been brought into being out of sheer joy.

As I realise (make real) my experience of oneness and enter into the peace of that experience, love arises spontaneously; it can do no other. As love arises it brings joy and joy arises spontaneously—it can do no other.

To experience this, what you have to do is allow yourself to be freed from the dominance of your ego's 'false self' by the simple practice of what I call soul-silence—exposing yourself to silent stillness. An experience of joy will then underlie many of your daily experiences, mundane though those experiences may be. You may become happy for all the wrong reasons but joy can only arise out of wholeness. Someone once said 'joy is its own justification'. If it is its own justification, it has a oneness built into it, tying it in with its sister fruits: peace and love.

Occasionally, in times of meditation or contemplation, I find myself suddenly overwhelmed with the joy of love for 'the one'. Tears stream down my face as I appreciate the grace of that loving presence which accepts me just as I am—warts and all. But you can't spend your life in ecstasy, nor is it good to seek such moments as if they are essential to the spiritual life. When they come, always unexpectedly, I cherish them, realising they are not a reward for anything I have done, but are pure grace.

Most usually my joy quietly bubbles just below the surface. Most usually, when I focus my awareness on what I'm doing: washing up, vacuuming the stairs or polishing the car—which Buddhists call mindfulness. That's when I find joy present. It is present in the company

48 The Upanishads, trans: Juan Mascaro, p111, Penguin Classics

of people. It is present in the warmth of sunshine and in the silence of a Quaker meeting. It was amazingly present as I lay waiting for the operation to remove one of my kidneys. Even in difficult circumstances I've discovered I know where to find the source of peace, love and joy. It's not difficult then to focus my awareness on the 'Tue Self' and experience these precious fruits of the spirit. That doesn't mean that life is one long joyous rapture with no blemishes at all, but it does mean that it's pretty damn good a lot of the time.

***

Although I experienced peace, love and joy during my intensely Christian phase, I found it to be a more common experience during what might be thought of as my post-Christian phase. It seemed to me appropriate, therefore, to revisit the New Testament and the teachings of Jesus in the light of my new understanding. I wondered whether I would find in the words of Jesus something of the truths I had learned from the *Upanishads* and *Tao Te Ching,* and whether the understanding gleaned from my many teachers would shed new light on the teaching of the New Testament.

Chapter Thirteen

The New Testament Re-examined

Once I'd more or less escaped from my paradigms concerning whatever it is we refer to as "God", and come to understand the purpose of mythology, I was able to take a less biased look at the foundation of my former faith, the New Testament. A stanza from Elliot's poem, *Little Gidding*, sums up this experience perfectly:

> *'We shall not cease from exploration*
> *And, at the end of all our exploring,*
> *We will arrive at where we started*
> *And know the place for the first time.'*

As I re-read the books and letters, from Matthew to Revelation, I discovered the same meanings which I'd discovered in the *Upanishads*, the *Bhagavad Gita* and *Tao Te Ching*. These books began to speak to me again, yet with a new voice. It was as if, all my life, I had been wearing bi-focal spectacles but only viewing spiritual matters through the reading lenses. Therefore I could see clearly only those things that were nearest to my own paradigms. Once I began to use the distance lenses as well, my spiritual world became a different place.

The Real New Testament

What we now call the New Testament was not finally approved as 'official' until the closing years of the fourth century C.E., and that in a meeting of the Roman Catholic church led by a Pope. Roman Catholicism was only one of many kinds of Christianity that existed by this time. None of my fundamentalist friends ever considered that it might be contradictory to regard as deserving of God's wrath those who had brought together the books of the New Testament.

I also never knew, or my mentors wilfully ignored the fact, that the letters of Paul were being circulated *before* the Gospels had been written.

Before their publication, experts suggest, a document containing the sayings of Jesus was all that had been recorded of his ministry.[49] A large body of opinion considers it is likely that the content of the Gospels were influenced by Paulian theology. It is probable that some of his ideas were 'retro-fitted' into the gospel stories to make their message consistent with Paul's new ideas.

History was repeating itself. The Old Testament had been put together to support the emerging 'Yahweh alone' theology of its day. Now the Gospel stories were being re-written to support Paul's 'proto-orthodox' theology. But naturally, we fundamentalists regarded the work of the textual critics as heretical, except, of course, the work of those who supported our point of view. However I came across a wealth of evidence to show that the New Testament should not be taken at face value.

Outside influences

Whether the influence of Zoroastrianism, beyond that already absorbed into Judaism during the captivity (see Chapter Seven), was present in Christianity from the outset, we cannot know. I suspect it came in with a number of other influences in the years after the death of Jesus. It certainly had an influence on the sect of the Pharisees who believed in the judgement and resurrection. And, of course, it was the cultural habit of the day to mythologize heroes, especially among the Greeks whose culture and language were widespread in Galilee.

As a former Pharisee, Paul would have been greatly influenced by teachings about the Messiah, judgement and resurrection, derived originally from the Persian religion which influenced the Jewish apocalyptic writers of the books of 1 Enoch and Jubilees. Even a cursory look at these books, written between the third and first centuries BCE, leaves the distinct impression that they laid the foundations for Christian thought about Satan, Hell, Judgement and Resurrection. Although they were never part of the Jewish or Christian canonical scriptures, they were

49 The Lost Gospel, Marcus Borg, Ulysses Press

in wide circulation among both Jews and Christians during the first few centuries of the Current Era.[50]

Although Jesus had preached against the behaviour of the Pharisees, their theology was nearer to Christianity than that of the other leading Jewish faction, the Sadducees. Indeed, after the destruction of Jerusalem only Pharisaical Judaism survived along with the Jewish sect that followed the teachings of Jesus. However, the Jews rarely spoke of a 'messiah' and usually referred to a king or high priest. Only Zoroastrians, Essenes (a Jewish sect) and Christians thought of a saviour in terms of a transcendent being in human form. Most Jews expected a military leader and a wise and just ruler.[51]

One important influence in early Christianity was the importation from Zoroastrianism of the 'Saviour's' virgin birth. Both Matthew and Luke refer to Mary as a virgin and Matthew quotes a passage from the 8th Century BCE, 'Yahweh Alone' prophet, Isaiah. In Chapter Seven Isaiah is prophesying to King Ahaz that his kingdom would be overthrown. He tells Ahaz to ask for any sign he likes, but Ahaz refuses. So Isaiah tells him that "God" himself will provide a sign. He then presents the world with one of the founding verses of Christianity; read in church at every carol service throughout the world:

> *'Therefore the Lord himself will give you a sign: The virgin will conceive and give birth to a son, and will call him Immanuel. He will be eating curds and honey when he knows enough to reject the wrong and choose the right, for before the boy knows enough to reject the wrong and choose the right, the land of the two kings you dread will be laid waste* [52]

Clearly, the original intention of these words was concerning a local matter, not a cosmic event such as the coming of the Messiah. What Isaiah is saying poetically was that from the time it takes to conceive, wean and

50 Lost Christianties, Bart L. Ehrman, Oxford University Press

51 Cosmos, Chaos and the World to Come, Norman Cohn, Yale University Press.

52 Isaiah 7:14:17

bring a child to know right from wrong, the enemies of Judah, at that time Rezin and Aram,[53] would be destroyed. Connecting it with the birth of Jesus really was stretching things a bit, so how was the connection made?

By the first century there had been a long tradition among Jewish rabbis of using the words of the Tanakh (the Old Testament) to discover spiritual truths that may have had little to do with the original context of the words. Such interpretation is called Midrash. One Rabbi said, *'Truly, you say to Scripture, 'Be silent while I am expounding!'* [54] The words of scripture, as well as being understood in its literal and historical context, could be used to illustrate a spiritual point metaphorically in current or even future context. It is easy to see how, in the tradition of Midrash, early Jewish Christians could begin to apply passages from the Tanakh, to the life of Jesus to corroborate their view of him as the Messaiah.

Biblical critics say the word 'virgin' is a mistranslation by Jerome. The word 'virgin' had appeared in a 3rd century BCE. Greek version of the Hebrew Bible.[55] Some argue that since the original Hebrew word was *almah* which means *young woman* or *maiden* it does not necessarily infer virginity. However, and to be fair, it might reasonably be assumed that a young unmarried women of this period would be a virgin. Yet this is beside the point. Starting with Matthew, Christians have obviously taken this passage out of context. Yet the tradition of a saviour to be born of a virgin had been an important part of the Zoroastrian culture which had so strongly influenced Judaism for nearly four centuries. However, it didn't find a candidate for Messiahship until the arrival of Mary's bastard, Jesus. Shocking as that term may seem, it was the inference of the words *'Isn't this Mary's son?'* in Mark 6:3. It was clearly the view of the people of Nazareth that Jesus was an illegitimate child or they would have said, 'Joseph's son'.

As my research continued I discovered Zoroastrians and Christians weren't the only ones to revere virgin birth. The concept had been part of

53 Isaiah 7:1
54 Sifra on Lev. xiii. 49
55 The Rejection of Pascal's Wager, Paul Tobin, Octavia & Co Press.

many religions on the Middle East for thousands of years. Here are just a few of dozens of instances:

- The virgin goddess Myrrha conceived the Greek god, Adonis.
- The Greek god Perseus, legendary founder of Mycenae, was born of the mortal virgin Danaë
- The Graeco-Roman god Dionysus, the god of wine, was born of the mortal virgin Semele.
- In Egypt Horus was born of the virgin Isis.
- Some first Century Romans believed Mithras was born of a virgin when lightning entered her.

There are many other parallels between the Mithraic myths and the stories told of Jesus. He appears to have started out as a Zoroastrian mythic figure who was changed into a bull-slaying god. Many aspects of his myth run parallel with the Jesus myth: One of his names was 'Lord of Light'*; he was sent as a saviour to deliver mankind; bread and wine were associated with him, and his birthday was 25th December. Early Christians were fully aware of the similarities and 2nd Century Christian theologian, Justin Martyr, dismissed them. He wrote:

> *'It having reached the Devil's ears that the prophets had foretold the coming of Christ, he set the Heathen Poets to bring forward a great many who should be called the sons of Jove. The Devil laying his scheme in this, to get men to imagine that the true history of Christ was of the same character as the prodigious fables related to the sons of Jove.'*

This is good logical rhetoric even if the theology is doubtful. In the 20th century I and my fellow Christians agreed with Justin Martyr and labelled any such connection with paganism as the deception of Satan. But it was nevertheless rhetoric, an 'art' which Plato regarded as largely an

* Also the designation of the Zoroastrian god Ahura Mazda

enemy of the truth. Incidentally, the idea of Satan also arose from Zoroastrianism, which makes all arguments about Christian doctrine become somewhat convoluted.

By the second century BCE the church widely held the doctrine of the virgin birth, or more accurately the virgin conception. Eventually the Roman Catholic and Eastern Orthodox churches concluded Mary must have remained a virgin *after* giving birth, despite the physical impossibility. They eventually went even further and claimed she herself was conceived 'immaculately' (though her mother didn't remain a virgin after the birth). Then, as recently as 1950, the Roman church officially substantiated the doctrine of the assumption of Mary—her bodily ascension into heaven. For me, this is a good demonstration of the kind of doctrinal 'patching up' theologians have to use to maintain their increasingly untenable position. You start with a virgin birth and end up with another deity.

Among Greeks the claim of the virgin birth clearly might have had some currency, but not among Jews. Was this linking of the fatherless child to a virgin birth a theological master-stroke which seemed to fulfil a midrash interpretation of Jewish prophecy *and* meet with the approval of Greek mythology? And if the virgin birth was such an important doctrine, I wondered, why didn't it appear uniformly throughout the New Testament? Neither Mark nor John mention the event in their Gospels, and such an omission is especially surprising in John. His Gospel emphasises the divinity of Jesus, and what greater evidence could there be of his divinity than that his literal father was the Almighty?

A further mystery is why Paul, who mentions virginity in relation to marriage and, metaphorically, of the relationship of the church to Christ, does not mention the virgin birth of Jesus in any of his letters. Although we may not have all of his letters, in those we have he writes of every other supernatural aspect of Jesus' life. The writers of the other epistles do not mention it either. It would therefore seem that the virgin birth was not as important to early Christians, even to Paul, as it is now.

There are many other mysteries surrounding the life of Jesus. If one regards the main tenet of the New Testament to be *mythological* rather than merely *logical* and its focus *meaning* rather than *fact,* then to examine them logically may be seen as a pointless exercise. But there are some mysteries which have helped me to understand the context of Jesus' teaching.

For instance, the title 'Jesus of Nazareth' may be a misnomer. It is, of course, possible that a tiny, undiscovered settlement of that name could have existed during Jesus' life time. There is certainly no archaeological or textual evidence for a town called Nazareth before the second century CE.[56] Neither the great Jewish historian, Josephus, nor the thorough and methodical Roman record keepers of the first century CE mention such a place. Most commonly it is believed that 'Nazareth' may be a corruption of the word 'Nazorean', a sect of the Essenes. This connection would probably not have been popular among Paulian Christians, which may explain its corruption to Nazareth and Nazarene. Other experts suggest it may have been the name of an area of the great Essene fortress at Masada. Among all this speculation there is a nagging connection with the Essenes, and there are some undeniable similarities between their beliefs and the teachings and behaviour of Jesus.

This Jewish messianic sect thrived during the first century CE. and Josephus records that they existed in their thousands. In common with Jesus, they baptised initiates, underwent self-denial and had beliefs about the end-days (the apocalypse) which they thought to be imminent. Like Jesus and his disciples, they strictly observed the Law. Further evidence of Jesus' connection with the Essenes has come from a possible recent solution to a theological argument which has run for centuries, if not millennia. In John's gospel Jesus was already under arrest and on trial by the time of the 'preparation of the Passover':[57] However, in the other gospels, Jesus and his disciples are celebrating the Passover supper *before* the betrayal and trial.[58] How could this be? The solution appears to

56 *James the Brother of Jesus,* R. Eisenman, New York: Penguin Books, 1997, p. 952

57 John 19:14

58 Mark 14

depend on the calendar used to calculate the time of the Passover. It had been the Jewish custom, based on the injunction of Leviticus 23:5, to calculate it on the Lunar calendar, as Christians do for Easter. However, from the evidence of the Dead Sea Scrolls, the Essenes used the Solar calendar to calculate the Passover, and ate the meal a day earlier and without lamb. Certainly there is no mention of lamb being present at the last supper in any of the Gospels, although there is a reference to the sacrifice of a lamb in Luke.

If Jesus did have a connection with the Essenes, it must have ended before his ministry began, because he did not behave like a typical Essene during his ministry. For instance, his reply to the Pharisees, when they asked him whether they should pay taxes to Rome, was to ask them to produce a coin. He then asked them whose image was on the coin. They replied, 'Caesar's'. Jesus told them to 'Give to Caesar what is Caesar's.' For Essenes there was no question in their minds. They were adamantly against the Roman occupation and would not have countenanced paying anything to Rome.

Jesus' ideas about what he called 'the kingdom of God' not only contradicted the behaviour and teaching of the Pharisees and Sadducees, but of the Essenes and every other religious movement in the Palestine of his day. In modern jargon we'd call it 'blue sky thinking'. For Jesus the kingdom was a spiritual experience within. For his contemporaries it was to do with the land of Israel, and Jerusalem in particular. Despite all this it seems possible that Essene teaching strongly influenced Jesus and his cousin John, at least prior to the beginning of his ministry in Galilee. This was especially so in their teaching of non-violence.

Yet another aspect of the story of Jesus is being brought to light by modern scholars. It appears that Galilee wasn't the rural backwater I always imagined it to be. Like Samaria, to the south-west, it had been part of the Northern Kingdom destroyed by the Assyrians in the 8th Century BCE. The population was made up of indigenous people and Jews, Greeks and Romans. Indeed, southern Galilee was culturally Greek or Greco-Roman to a large extent. The cities of Tiberius and Sepphoris were both built in the Greco-Roman style and most people in the south of the district were bi-lingual, speaking both Greek and Aramaic. Gadara, where Jesus cast out demons from a madman, was also Greek, in fact it had its own schools of philosophy and was a centre for those of the Cynic School.[59] There are so many parallels between the philosophy of the Cynics and the teachings of Jesus, it is hard to resist the thought that they too must have influenced him. Wikipedia says:

> *'Their philosophy was that the purpose of life was to live a life of virtue in agreement with nature. This meant rejecting all conventional desires for wealth, power, health, and fame, and by living a simple life free from all possessions. As reasoning creatures, people could gain happiness by rigorous training and by living in a way which was natural for humans. They believed that the world belonged equally to everyone, and that suffering was caused by false judgements of what was valuable and by the worthless customs and conventions which surrounded society. Many of these thoughts were later absorbed into Stoicism.'*

Paul too had a connection with Greek philosophy. He was brought up in Tarsus, a centre of Stoicism. He even quoted a Stoic philosopher when he preached in Athens, saying, '*In him we live and move and have our being.*'

Another mystery may illustrate how Paulian theology may have been inserted into the synoptic gospels. The Jews were forbidden to eat or drink blood. The Law states quite clearly:

> *'If any man of the house of Israel or of the strangers that sojourn among them eats any blood, I will set my face against that person who eats blood, and will cut him off from among his people.'*[60]

59 The Lost Gospel, pp 51-68, Burton L. Mack, Element

60 Leviticus 17:10

Yet according to Matthew's Gospel, Jesus takes a forbidden dietary practice and uses it as a metaphor for the spiritual life he espouses. In the Gospel of John he says:

> *'Truly, truly, I say to you, unless you eat the flesh of the Son of Man and drink his blood, you have no life in you.'*[61]

The thought of 'eating' blood, even symbolically, would surely have been an abhorrence to a practising Jew. How much more the thought of cannibalism? Was there a Romano-Greek influence here? Their temple rituals involved a lot of blood. Could such statements be a Paulian insertion to emphasise Paul's teaching that Jesus' death was a sacrifice for sin? It was the practice that the meat of the sacrificed lamb was eaten at the Passover. This teaching was the lynch pin of Paul's gospel, yet I cannot find any teaching by Jesus that directly refers to his death as being a sacrifice for sin. Had he taught this, why were his disciples thrown into confusion after the crucifixion? The emphasis of Jesus' gospel was practical healing and caring, and central to it was that the kingdom of "God" was within. Or was this doctrine of sacrifice designed to make Paul's teaching appeal to the Gentiles?

The Gospel of Jesus or The Gospel of Paul?

I find it very strange that although there are plenty of references to 'the gospel' 'or the good news' in the Synaptic Gospels (Matthew, Mark and Luke), there is little indication of what the content of that message was. The word 'gospel' itself is not a precise term. We've come to use it in reference to the content of the first four books of the New Testament, but the Old English *god spell*, simply means good discourse, tidings or news—a direct translation of the Greek word *euangelos* made up of *eu* (good or beautiful) and *angelos* (message—angels are simply messengers.) There is no clear cut definition in any of the synoptic gospels of what the content of 'The Gospel' actually is.

---

61 John 6:53

So when Jesus sent the disciples out to preach in Mark Chapter Six what did they preach? Primarily, it seems, they were sent on a largely practical mission to heal the sick and cast out demons. Secondarily, their message was vaguely something to do with what Jesus referred to as 'the Kingdom of God'. All we know is that he regarded the kingdom as being something inner, not visible. It seems it's a place within each one of us by default, not something we have to obtain. Access to the kingdom is by simply changing our minds about the way we live. Jesus' gospel is emphatically about something people were expected to *do.* It had nothing whatsoever to do with a doctrine they had to believe. Neither, strange to relate, is there any direct reference in the Gospels to the idea that sin demanded a human sacrifice in order to expiate it. John the Baptist preached a similar message to Jesus, asking people to submit to baptism for the forgiveness of sin. Jesus forgave sin on a more casual basis. So, if sin could be forgiven *before* the crucifixion, how come the crucifixion should later become the means by which sin can be forgiven by 'God'?

I'm sure the first thing that will spring to some theological minds is that "God" anticipated the sacrifice of his son, but the Bible makes no reference to this. Maybe some will call on the Abraham and Isaac story to conjecture that "God" always anticipated such a situation, but it's very easy to make Old Testament events fit the Jesus story in retrospect. Right from the outset Isaiah was quoted widely, and completely out of context on all counts, to explain the Jesus phenomena. But it's no longer acceptable to take a text out of context and make it into a pretext. In a sense, we know too much, and to go back to a belief system that demands we accept doctrines which are no longer viable would be a seriously retrograde step. The gospel of Jesus was *so* simple. Change your mind, love the "God" that lives within you and your neighbour as yourself. That's it.

Paulianity?

In my fundamentalist era I'd thought the early disciples were Christians like me. When I started to speak in tongues, heard and uttered 'prophecies' and witnessed healing, this reinforced the idea. It was a bit of a shock to discover that, before Paul appeared on the scene, the early disciples thought of themselves, not as Christians at all, but as Jews, albeit rather special Jews. It is even possible they didn't think of Jesus as the Messiah [62]. They didn't call themselves 'Christians' but 'Followers of the Way' [63], and had no intention of going 'into all the world and preach the good news to all creation [64] but were content to remain at home. This leads me to speculate whether this injunction may have been another late insertion in the Gospel of Mark.

Scholars had been speculating about a source document for the synoptic gospels since the early 1800s. In 1945 discoveries of manuscripts at Nag Hammadi included the Gospel of Thomas which contained sayings analogous to the synoptic gospels. New and better analytical tools revealed an original source of the sayings of Jesus hidden in the Gospels which became known as 'Q', for Quelle the German word for source. This collection of sayings, primarily about ethical behaviour, follows a traditional genre found in the middle east. To these were added commentaries by the writers of the gospels and later were added apocalyptic references similar to those found in the Babylonian books of Enoch 1 and Jubilees. Finally Mark was written and these collections were incorporated into the Gospels of Matthew and Luke. If this is so, could the late insertions have been the result of Paul's influence? Paul's letters are full of apocalyptic references; in fact, his teachings were the main source of my fundamentalist understanding of the judgement and second coming of Jesus.

After Paul's apparently miraculous conversion on the Damascus road, he became as passionate an advocate of the followers of Jesus as he had been an adversary. His influence was immediately intense and widespread, though never universal. One of Paul's controversial views was that the message of the death and resurrection of Jesus was for all people, not just Jews. This idea was resisted by many of the original disciples. Some did accept the idea but demanded that all converts should be circumcised. But

62 The Lost Gospel, Burton L. Mack, Element.

63 Acts 9:2

64 Mark 16:15

Paul would have none of it. Such matters were the cause of many tussles he had with the original disciples and the new church. He wrote to the Galatians:

> *'But when Cephas [Simon Peter] came to Antioch, I opposed him to his face, because he stood condemned. For before certain men came from James, he was eating with the Gentiles; but when they came he drew back and separated himself, fearing the circumcision party.* [65]

James, the brother of Jesus, was the leading apostle in Jerusalem. The friction between him and Paul must surely have been greater than Luke's sanitized version in the book of Acts.[66] James and the other disciples observed the Torah strictly and demanded circumcision. Paul claimed it was the death of Jesus alone, not the Law, which redeemed believers.[67] These views are in diametric opposition; they are not slight misunderstandings. If Paul was right, it's strange that Jesus obviously had not addressed the issue more clearly with those who were close to him throughout his ministry. But then, Jesus thought of himself as a faithful Jew, not the founder of a new religion. It was Paul who founded the new religion when he won the argument with James and the circumcision party. It was not long after his acceptance among the 'Followers of the Way' that the believers began to develop an identity which separated them from Jews. At Antioch (now Antakya in Southern Turkey) they first began to call themselves 'Christians'.[68]

Paul's master stroke was to develop a theology that explained the death of Jesus, while at the same time linking it directly to the Jewish Old Testament and the Law and, at the same time, making it acceptable to Greeks. His doctrine that the death of Jesus was a once and for all sacrifice for sin, closed the book on the Law and allowed Gentiles to be equal

65 Galatians 2:11-12
66 Acts 15
67 Galatians 5
68 Acts 11:26

partners in the growing church. It also relieved Jewish members of the burdens of their religion, with its complex observances. Jesus, as Paul was at pains to point out, fulfilled the law; they were no longer under the law but under grace. It was a deeply meaningful solution to what could have become an intractable problem and Christians, both Jewish and Gentile alike, readily took it on board. Paul also evolved the Zoroastrian concept of the resurrection of the dead and The Judgement of the Last Day, making Christ, embodied in Jesus, the judge and linking the current political predicament with the imminent return of the Messiah.

The more I thought around this issue the more I began to realise that Paul's teaching about Jesus ignores the gospels and the sayings of Q that preceded them. That's not altogether to be unexpected, since they weren't written down until after Paul's letters were in circulation. The whole emphasis of his letters is on the death of Jesus as a sacrifice for sin, his resurrection and his coming again to judge the living and dead. This makes me even more convinced that the few references in the gospels themselves, which are taken by Christians as contiguous with Paul's teaching, must have been retrofitted to give Paul's doctrines some semblance of historical authority. But by this, I don't mean that anyone was being deliberately devious or dishonest. It was the way the people handled information in that era. Six of the thirteen epistles of Paul recorded in the New Testament are widely considered to have been written by someone other than Paul (pseudonymous). Naturally, this is disputed. But 1st century writers were not averse to ascribing the authorship of documents, that they themselves had written, to someone whom they respected.

My view now is that the New Testament is far from inerrant. Apart from inaccuracies and contradictions, a lot has been lost in translation. Trying to impose a narrow meaning on any word or passage is doomed to failure linguistically, quite apart from spiritually. Yet, again, that's not to say its writers were insincere and trying to deliberately mislead. Theirs was an era when little was understood about the properties of the physical and natural world. Heaven was on the other side of the vast blue dome which sat like a gigantic warming dish covering the earth. The communication modes of 'mythos' and 'logos' had equal value, even though sometimes the distinctions became blurred. Most people, most of the time, understood when a thing should be taken as metaphor and when as fact. Paul's passion and sincerity shine through his writing and, although I find much that can no longer be credible, there is much in it that I shall always cherish. He seems to have been at his best when speaking as a mystic. As a theologian, he was brilliant but dangerous, as I think history shows.

There have been many times when a warmth has arisen within me when I've discovered meaning in a passage of the Bible. Now I recognise it as the same warmth that arises in me as I read the *Bhagavad Gita*, the *Upanishads*, the *Tao Teh Ching* or any other spiritual work. It is present when I ponder passages from the Buddhist *Vinaya* or the work of poets like Rumi, Wordsworth or T.S. Eliot. I recognise it when I read Simone Weil, Eckhart Tolle or Richard Rohr. Meaning is in me. The Bible is one of many buckets I can use to draw it into awareness.

Chapter Fourteen

The Teaching of Jesus Revisited

From early in my Christian experience I understood Jesus' teaching to have been markedly different from the received ideas of his day. Why else would the religious powers have wanted so often to 'take up stones' against him and ultimately to crucify him? However, because I had been brought up in a Christian culture, what those around me presumed to be Jesus' teaching seemed quite normal. It had never occurred to me that the teaching had degenerated into unquestioned orthodoxy over the centuries.

All of we 'believers' seemed to have accepted that Christianity represents standards to which we should aspire but, since we were fallen humans, were unlikely to achieve. For some, this was a licence to ignore the teachings much of the time. For others it was an opportunity to gather guilt and act 'humble'. It wasn't until I began to see Jesus' teachings in a wider context that I realised how radically different his message was from my own understanding. Indeed, I was soon to discover that much of what I had formerly believed was a mirror image of the truth. It was another case of seeing in a mirror and getting things the wrong way around.

What Jesus taught is the opposite of almost all religious teaching of his day. The Jews believed in an earthly kingdom, Jesus spoke of a kingdom within and this even confused his disciples.[69] The Jews believed in strict observance of the Law; Jesus taught purity of heart was not an outcome of observance, but a pre-requisite. He told his disciples to offer sacrifice *because* their motives were pure, not in order to become pure. [70] Orthodoxy believed observance of the Law meant excluding all that was impure and unclean—lepers, tax gatherers and prostitutes etc. Jesus included all of them among his followers. [71] The priests believed the solution to Rome was violent insurrection; Jesus taught them to take the path of non-violence and to love their enemies. [72]

---

69 Mark 10:35-38
70 Matthew 5:23,24
71 Matthew 9:11
72 Matthew 5:38-42

His teaching is full of paradoxes. He says to find your life, you have to lose it; to become mature enough to enter the kingdom of Heaven, you have to become a little child; to receive, you have to give; to be forgiven, you have to forgive; to overcome, you have to yield; to love your neighbour, you have to love yourself; that the meek, not the powerful, shall inherit the earth. For him the truth was the opposite of many things people at large held dear. And that's still true today.

Mainstream Jews believed in a largely impersonal, intangible "God" whose presence (Shekinah) was behind the veil in the Holy of Holies, but whose actual presence was in Heaven. This was, of course, the Bronze Age warrior god I spoke of earlier; one whom they expected would meet violence with violence. Being a god of wrath, he needed much propitiation, which resulted in the mass slaughter of animals brought to the temple for sacrifice. On the positive side, this process brought the people together and gave them a sense of unity. But their unity centred around being a nation called into being by "God" through Abraham. Jesus told the Jews that "God" could raise children to Abraham from the very stones if he wished—which didn't go down too well in the Sanhedrin. And he introduced them to a more personal "God"; one he referred to as *Abba*, 'father', or, as some interpret this Aramaic word, 'Daddy'.

I began to realise that much of what I had learned from my fellow Christians also turned out to be a mirror image of the truth. I had thought of "God" as a unique being, yet Jesus spoke of our being one with him and he being one with the father. In other words Jesus did not appear to consider "God" as a unique being but as 'being' itself. The import of Jesus' statement, 'I and the Father are one,' is that without the being of "God", I have no being. I had thought of this oneness as being unique to Jesus, yet, according to John, at the end of his ministry Jesus prayed that the disciples might be one with the Father just as he was. [73] It's important to note that, again, Jesus didn't ask that they might *become* one, but that they realised they *were* one with the Father. However, it seems they had not entered into the experience at that point, otherwise there would be no

73 John 17:11

reason for the prayer, and this may account, in part, for the disarray they found themselves in after the crucifixion.

This oneness, this total unity of being, I'd learned about in the Upanishads. Now I discovered it to be the very core of Jesus' message. In the *Isha Upanishad* it says,

> *'Who sees all beings in his own Self, and his own Self in all beings, loses all fear.'*

Here, the Self is what I have referred to earlier as the 'True Self'. The *Isha* revealed to me the truth of Jesus: there is no distinction between "God" and my 'True Self'. This is why, when the Pharisees accused Jesus of claiming to be "God", he didn't deny it but quoted a passage from Psalm 82 , *'Is it not written in your Law, 'I have said you are gods'?'* He then went on to support his arguments by saying,

> *'If he called them "gods," to whom the word of God came—and the Scripture cannot be broken—what about the one whom the Father set apart as his very own and sent into the world? Why then do you accuse me of blasphemy because I said, "I am God's Son"?'*[74]

In quoting this scripture, Jesus shows himself as an example of what he regarded to be generally true. He is saying that not only he, but all those 'to whom the word of God had come'; all those who had become enlightened by the awakening of the word (the power of "God", not the scripture) in their hearts were gods: they are all 'one with the father'.

As a fundamentalist Christian I had believed that what separated me from "God", what kept me from being one with the father, was original sin. Until Jesus came again, I had believed, I had to manage my tendency towards sinfulness with the help of "God". Only when, as Paul put it, *'this*

74 John 10:34

corruptible had put on incorruption' [75] at the Resurrection could I be fully free of it. I had, therefore, never considered something which I later became aware of in reading some of the Vedic scriptures: the existence of that 'original goodness' I spoke of earlier. Such a concept was another mirror image of what I had grown up to believe. Could I find such an idea among the teachings of Jesus?

I didn't have far to look. At the end of the Sermon on the Mount in Matthew Chapter Five is an amazing command: *'Be perfect as your Father is perfect.'* As I examined this verse more closely, I realised that, as in the passage in John, Jesus didn't say, 'Become'. That would have required the Greek text to use a quite different word, *ginomai*. No, the text has Jesus use the verb 'to be', *eimi*. In other words, be perfect right now; realise that perfection (the kingdom of Heaven) lies within you. I don't have to do anything to obtain that perfection, that original goodness. My perfection doesn't depend on getting good enough, saying enough prayers, repenting fully enough, denying enough. It doesn't depend on me at all but on the 'True Self'. And since I'm one with the 'True Self', that essence of perfection is always within me whether I recognise it or not.

Jesus said, *'Blessed are the pure in heart, for they shall see God.'* [76] Something similar is echoed in the Chandogya Upanishad, where it says,

> *'The Self, who can be realised by the pure in heart, who is life, light, truth, space . . .who is joy abiding—this is the Self dwelling in my heart.'* [77]

As a Christian I had been preaching about the need for Jesus to *come into* the hearts of my audiences, but I never, ever understood the full implications of what I was saying. I had understood it as part of the process of conversion. It was about being 'born again' by saying a prayer of acceptance. Not until that transaction had taken place, I had believed, was salvation granted. Jesus never taught that and I never understood that

75 1 Corinthians 15:53

76 Matthew 5:8

77 Chandogya III 14.2, translation by Eknath Easwaran, Arkana

every single one of the congregation whom I had urged to 'accept Jesus as their personal saviour' had actually *already been accepted* by "God". They were already one with him. All they had to do was to wake up to the fact. What I had been preaching was a mirror image of what Jesus taught.

The total oneness we have with the divine we have *by default.* When Jesus expressed his desire that his disciples *'may be one, as we are one',* it was for their realization of this experience he was asking. Paul expressed to the Galatians his experience of oneness like this: *'It is no longer I that live but Christ lives in me.'* [78] A similar idea is expressed in the *Shvetashvatara Upanishad*: *'Know him to be enshrined in your heart always.'* [79] Note the "always". Later in the same passage it says, *'He is the inner Self of all, hidden like a little flame in the heart.'*

I had often spoken of Jesus as being "in my heart," but had always conceived this presence as something separate from me, rather like an 'app' on a mobile phone. From the way Paul expressed his experience, maybe he thought of it like that too. Being the kind of Christian I was, I thought of my body as 'the flesh'. I understood this to be 'consigned to evil'. But eventually I discovered the 'flesh' refers to the unredeemed mind, not the body at all, and for 'unredeemed', I guess you can read 'unrealised'.

I now realise that Jesus' call to "follow me" meant every aspect of his relationship with "God" was mine by default. If my birthright as a human being is to be a child of "God", then I could not become one with "God" because I already was one with "God". Whatever it is I refer to when I use the term "God" is not separated from anything in the cosmos, but an integral and co-creative aspect of it. I simply had to realise, become conscious, of what I am. This realisation is illustrated well by an old Indian animal-legend I found in my copy of 'The Joseph Campbell Companion'.

A heavily pregnant tigress, who was desperately hungry, went hunting among a flock of goats. The agile goats all got away, but the effort was too

78 Galatians 2:20

79 Shvetashvatara verse 12, translation by Eknath Easwaran, Arkana

great for the tigress. She gave birth to a solitary cub and died. When the goats returned to their clearing, they found a pitiful little lump of fur that had crawled away from its dead mother in search of food. Being good parents, a foster mum came forward and gave suckle to the cub. Soon he grew into a young tiger, though a bit on the skinny side because, living among goats, he only ate grass.

One day, his tiger instinct led him to wander off into the jungle alone and there he met an adult male tiger.

'Who are you?' demanded the male ferociously.

'Baa,' replied the young one.

'What's that supposed to mean?' asked the male tiger, indignantly.

'Baa,' said the young tiger, 'Please, Sir, I'm a goat.'

'Humbug!' exclaimed the adult male. 'You're a tiger like me. Come, I'll show you.'

As in Hans Christian Anderson's story of the ugly duckling, the young tiger was taken to a still pool where he could see his face beside that of the adult male. (It is in stillness we discover the truth about ourselves and it is in the presence of the mature that we mature.) Then the male tiger took him off into the jungle to his den where there were the remains of a recently slaughtered gazelle. Joseph Campbell relates the rest of the story like this: *'Taking a chunk of this bloody stuff, the big tiger says, "Open your face."*

The little one backs away [and says], *'I'm a vegetarian.'*

'None of that nonsense,' says the big fellow, and he shoves a piece of meat down the little one's throat. He gags on it. The [Native American] text says, "As all do on true doctrine." '[80]

The moral, says Campbell, is that we're all tigers living here as goats. Orthodoxy wants to keep us that way—part of a herd, biddable, leadable and kept in a corral. The mirror image of the orthodox is the individual in a deep personal relationship with the divine (whatever the individual understands that to be). Jesus was not part of the 'system'. He said he had

80 The Joseph Campbell Companion, Diane K. Osbon, Harper Perennial

nowhere to lay his head.[81] He worked and lived, mostly 'outside' the religious establishment and called his followers to be prepared to suffer as outcasts.

Those of us who begin to walk in the light of the True Self reach a point when we realise we are surrounded by tigers who think they are goats! What do we do about that? Do we try to conform or launch out into the unknown? This was exactly the situation Jesus was in. During his short years of ministry, a 'crowd' regularly gathered around him and he regularly left them to be alone or with his disciples. The crowd were a nuisance, often restricting access to genuine seekers, like the paralysed man forced to be let down by his friends from the roof into the presence of Jesus.[82] Yet he also touched individuals within the crowd, sometimes with apparently accidental result, such as the healing of the woman with the emission.[83] But in the end it was the 'crowd' which called for Barabbas to be released, rather than Jesus.

Slowly it dawned on me that the 'Gospel' is about "God" dwelling, not in a temple or in heaven, but in the heart of each one of us. This is not about doctrine or belief but about a palpable experience revealed in peace that passes all understanding, unconditional love and pure joy. As I pointed out in the previous chapter, this was the only gospel the disciples could have preached in Jesus' lifetime and they expressed it in sharing all things in common, healing the sick and caring for the poor. Paul recommended this kind of action too but he never referred to oneness with the father. The nearest he got was to speak of *'Christ within me, the hope of glory'*—yet this was a glory that was future and dependent on the physical return of Jesus, not a palpable experience now. Paul's ministry is focused primarily on the Christ as revealed in Jesus. He related the death of Jesus to the traditional Jewish sacrifice for sin, but if, as Jesus told his followers, the kingdom is (already) within you, what need is there for a sacrifice? Jesus' ministry, on the other hand, wasn't about himself; it was totally focused on the Father.

81 Matthew 8:20
82 Mark 2:3-5
83 Matthew 9:21,22

If the death of Jesus was not about a sacrifice for sin, and Jesus never said it was, what was it about? There is a vitally important element in Jesus' teaching which Paul never speaks of—non-attachment. I express it that way rather than 'detachment' because the latter word has derived some negative connotations. In modern parlance it infers a cold, inscrutable attitude, whereas non-attachment is far from that. The key to this I found in Matthew Five, which is all about non-violence. What drew me to this was reading the Bhagavad Gita, Gandhi's favourite scripture.

On first reading the Bhagavad Gita, probably the world's greatest teaching on non-attachment, I was confused. The book begins with the warrior Arjuna, supported by his mighty army, facing an equally mighty army of his cousins, uncles and teachers. He doesn't want to kill any of them and is pleading with the god Krishna, who happens to be his chariot driver, for some way to avoid the conflict. At first sight it seems Krishna is saying, forget these are your uncles, cousins and teachers, your job as a warrior is to kill them. To someone like me, convinced that the spiritual path is one of non-violence, this didn't seem to be consistent with spiritual values. But the actual lesson seems to be this: Do what it is right for you to do, and do not attach yourself to the outcomes. This is how the writer of the Bhagavad Gita has Krishna express it:

> *'You have the right to work, but never to the fruit of work. You should never engage in action for the sake of reward, nor should you long for inaction. Perform work in this world, Arjuna, as a man established within himself—without selfish attachments, and alike in success and defeat . . .'*[84]

Matthew has Jesus say something with a similar import in Chapter Six of his gospel:

> *'Therefore I tell you, do not worry about your life, what you will eat or drink; or about your body, what you will wear. Is not life*

84 Bhagavad Gita, Discourse II:47, Trans Eknath Easwaran, Harper Perennial

more important than food, and the body more important than clothes?'[85]

In other words, don't be attached to desire for food, drink and clothing that some people assume is the sole reason for working. Focus on what you're doing. As Paul says, '*. . .whether you eat or drink or whatever you do, do it all for the glory of God.'* If we focus on the outcome of what we do, like business people focusing solely on the bottom line, we'll miss the important aspect of what we're really doing: serving others. The Bhagavad Gita gives us the theology of non-attachment, but the words of Jesus in Matthew give us a most practical illustration of the principles and how they may be worked out in everyday life:

'You have heard that it was said, 'Eye for eye, and tooth for tooth.' But I tell you, Do not resist an evil person. If someone strikes you on the right cheek, turn to him the other also. And if someone wants to sue you and take your tunic, let him have your cloak as well. If someone forces you to go one mile, go with him two miles. Give to the one who asks you, and do not turn away from the one who wants to borrow from you.'[86]

It's so easy to react negatively to the impositions of others. Jesus doesn't here judge whether those impositions are good or bad. What he's concerned with is what we call the ego. We can now understand that it is the ego, through its false self, which is offended, insulted or simply 'put out' by the impositions. I discovered I had to let the impositions do their work in me—put my false self to death—so I can be 'without selfish attachments and alike in success and defeat'. Initially, this is a painful process—death usually is.

But as the chains that anchored me to desire and fear began to weaken, I found that it became easier and easier to be non-attached. Under my

85 Matthew 6:25

86 Matthew 5:38-42

former belief system I had to 'fight the good fight' to maintain any semblance of detachment. In the non-attached state of awareness I found through the practice of soul-silence, I found I had less and less to desire other than the love of the divine, and little to fear but failing to experience it. As the practice of non-attachment progresses, tasks are performed in joy. Joy is found in realising it is not I, the ego's false self, who is performing the task, but the Self, the Christ within me. Gandhi says a service provided without joy is of no use either to the server or the served, and he served others by cleaning out their cesspits.

I've no doubt the principle of non-attachment influenced Rudyard Kipling when he wrote his poem 'If'. He had lived among Hindus for many years (his first language was Hindi) and this poem sums up the principle perfectly.

If you can keep your head when all about you
Are losing theirs and blaming it on you,
If you can trust yourself when all men doubt you,
But make allowance for their doubting too;
If you can wait and not be tired by waiting,
Or being lied about, don't deal in lies,
Or being hated, don't give way to hating,
And yet don't look too good, nor talk too wise:

If you can dream - and not make dreams your master;
If you can think - and not make thoughts your aim;
If you can meet with Triumph and Disaster
And treat those two impostors just the same;
If you can bear to hear the truth you've spoken
Twisted by knaves to make a trap for fools,
Or watch the things you gave your life to, broken,
And stoop and build 'em up with worn-out tools:

If you can make one heap of all your winnings
And risk it on one turn of pitch-and-toss,
And lose, and start again at your beginnings
And never breathe a word about your loss;
If you can force your heart and nerve and sinew
To serve your turn long after they are gone,
And so hold on when there is nothing in you
Except the Will which says to them: 'Hold on!'

If you can talk with crowds and keep your virtue,
Or walk with Kings - nor lose the common touch,
if neither foes nor loving friends can hurt you,
If all men count with you, but none too much;
If you can fill the unforgiving minute
With sixty seconds' worth of distance run,
Yours is the Earth and everything that's in it,
And - which is more - you'll be a Man, my son!

(And it should go without saying it's equally true that 'you'll be a woman, my daughter!')

The Edwardians interpreted the subject of Kipling's poem as about the 'stiff upper lip' and all that. They largely missed the point he was making about non-attachment in relation to fear and desire. The English 'stiff upper lip' is merely repression. Non-attachment is about letting go and it takes consistent mindfulness over a long period to even begin to realise the non-attached position. There's also an important pre-condition for realising this kind of awareness— death. Not physical death, but death of the ego's false self, and this too was at the very heart of Jesus' message. It is stated most clearly in Matthew 16:24, where Jesus says,

'If anyone would come after me, he must deny himself and take up his cross and follow me.'

Entering fully into the experience of non-attachment is impossible without this precondition. The ego, which gets offended, feels proud and gets drawn hither and thither by fear and desire, has to be disempowered. Once this begins to happen, largely through the practice of soul-silence which brings the realisation that I am one with the Self, non-attachment can begin to be experienced. I say 'begin' because it's not something I've found I can leap into. I'm still learning day by day. Some days are better than others, but I'm beginning to recognise the signs that indicate I'm attached, and am learning to find my way back.

But there is a health warning among all this: non-attachment without love produces the inscrutable, unemotional caricature of the eastern mystic whom film directors like to portray. That's not detachment but indifference and is in sharp contrast to the loving and all-embracing openness of someone like the Dalai Llama, who also has a great sense of fun. It is something I find I have to let myself fall into, rather than arm myself with. It's about surrender and therefore also about faith, not in the impossible, but in the virtue of that which enables all things in love, and which itself perfectly embodies non-attachment.

All this led me to a new understanding of the point of the Cross. Could it be that, in allowing himself to be captured, charged and executed, Jesus was following his Father in being totally non-coercive and totally non-violent? After the Sermon on the Mount, he'd be a hypocrite if he resisted the evil person, even when that person came to take him to his death. Is this also why he gave no reply to the charges laid against him by the Sanhedrin? Maybe all this happened, not because he knew he had to die for our sins, but because it is not the nature of "God" to gain advantage by coercion or violence. Might this explain the reason why, in the Gospels, there are so few direct references to the death of Jesus as a sacrifice, and those that appear to be, or are interpreted as such, are generally oblique. Since the Gospels were written down after the Pauline letters, it would be a simple thing to retrofit Paulian theology into the text. Speculation, you say? Of course, but if "God" is as non-violent and non-coercive as Jesus so clearly taught, what alternative is there? Centuries before, Micah had said that "God" did not require sacrifice[87] and Jesus explicitly said that the rule 'an eye for an eye' was defunct. If we are to unconditionally forgive 'those who spitefully use us' as Jesus did, how could "God" behave less perfectly than that? To me, the demand for a penalty and a sacrifice for sin makes no sense any more. "God" is better than that.

Remember that last verse of Matthew Five: *'Be perfect as your Father is perfect.'* The sermon was not just about how we should behave as followers of Jesus. This is the way we will be once we realise our perfection in "God", because that's the way "God" is.

87 Micah 6:6-8

Chapter Fifteen

"God", Science and Creation

Throughout my 'religious era' I had always felt that scientists were my enemies. It was not that I disliked science. Just that scientists kept inconveniently discovering things which seemed to question the authenticity of my fundamentalist beliefs. Had Ken Ham's Creationist Museum, near Cincinnati, existed then I would have been one of its greatest enthusiasts.

When I began to look into the history of this anti-scientific attitude I discovered that the separation had been developing for well over a century —especially post-Darwin. On the extremely religious side were (and are) those whose paradigms are that evolution is the lie of Satan. They believe in the authoritative word of the Bible "God" which says that in six days He created the heaven and the earth and all that's in it. On the extremely scientific side are those whose paradigms arose out of Newtonian physics. This led to scientific-materialism (matter is all that matters), and extreme Darwinism (life is about the survival of the fittest). Perhaps it's because I'm a Libran I prefer a balanced position. I find polarised views tend usually to be wrong and reality lies somewhere between the two.

I'd read the theological arguments and they seemed to assume that the only authority that could be reliable was the Bible. That, of course, was based on the presumption that it was the divinely inspired word of "God", and the only authority for that presumption was the book itself! We had interpreted the term 'word of God' to refer to scripture but, when those words were written, the Bible didn't exist. Read carefully, no reference to 'the word of God' in the Bible is a reference to the Bible.

Considerable contortions were performed by fundamentalist Christians who were scientists by profession to show how science could be reconciled with the Bible. I read such explanations and watched Moody Bible Institute films with much enthusiasm. Later I found that many scientists are more honest and open to mystery than most theologians. Bertrand Russell said,

> *'Physics is mathematical, not because we know so much about the physical world, but because we know so little. It is only the mathematical properties we can discover.'* Fred Hoyle (1915-2001) went so far as to write: *'Would you not say to yourself, 'Some super-calculating intellect must have designed the properties of the carbon atom, otherwise the chance of my finding such an atom through the blind forces of nature would be utterly minuscule.' Of course you would. A common sense interpretation of the facts suggests that a super-intellect has monkeyed with physics, as well as with chemistry and biology, and that there are no blind forces worth speaking about in nature. The numbers one calculates from the facts seem to me so overwhelming as to put this conclusion almost beyond question.'*[88]

Sir James Jeans (1877—1946) said that the universe begins to look more like a great thought than a great machine. Einstein seems to have agreed though he never fully accepted the idea and, despite considerable effort, never repudiated it either. However, he did say,

> *'The most beautiful and profound emotion we can experience is the sensation of the mystical. It is the source of all true science.'*[89]

The advances in quantum physics and cosmology since then have only confirmed that we live within a conscious, intelligent universe of which Earth, or Gaia as James Lovelock calls her, is but one tiny speck. Life depends on many millions of interdependent 'coincidences'. Belief that they can all be down to chance alone makes believing the Bible a much smaller step of blind faith. A fraction more oxygen in the atmosphere and everything would burn up, a fraction more nitrogen and everything would freeze. A fraction more gravity and everything would cluster into one big lump, a fraction less and everything would fly apart. And so the list could

88 The Universe: Past and Present Reflections, Fred Hoyle, *Engineering and Science*, Nov. 1981.
89 New York Times obituary, 1955

go on to fill hundreds of thousands of pages. Life depends totally on millions of phenomena, each of which have to exist in fine balance with the other. For a few of these phenomena to arise coincidentally would be a degree of chance of considerable magnitude. For thousands of them to arise would be incalculable. Not that I rule out random chance entirely. Rather, it looks very much as if the dice has been consistently loaded to ensure, in the long run, not a particular outcome, but a particular *kind* of outcome. In other words, where an opportunity to weight the dice arises, the dice get weighted— despite what Einstein said about "God" not playing dice with the universe.

I was surprised to discover it's even possible to observe such rolling of a loaded dice. It's an effect which scientists call 'seriality' and you can carry out this experiment yourself—if you can spare the time and have the patience. Let me explain.

You will need a watch, a pencil and some paper. Take them along to your nearest shopping mall and begin by counting the number of people in each five or ten minute periods who are wearing, say, brown shoes. (Now you know I'm crazy). Then go on to count people carrying newspapers, who are wearing something blue or have hats. After a while, if you're patient, you'll discover patterns emerging among your figures. Although you'd expect the distribution of brown shoes, hats or people with papers to be totally random, they're not—not totally. You'll find little clusters of people wearing brown shoes—two, then perhaps four. It's as if someone is standing at the door to the mall saying, 'Brown shoes next, please,' and holding up those with different coloured shoes, until a little group of brown-shod people has got in. And before you write me off as completely mad, a scientist named Paul Kammerer actually observed this happening for weeks on end to prove his theory of seriality.[90] This work was regarded as 'interesting' by Einstein and influenced Jung's ideas on synchronicity.

Shopkeepers know all about this phenomenon. Suddenly, and quite unpredictably, a shop will fill up with people—usually just as the assistant wants to tidy the stock! Then the shop will be empty for a while. This may

90 The Roots of Coincidence, Arthur Koestler, Picador

happen several times a day, interspersed with periods when a few people will amble in or the shop will be crowded. A café might have a run on BLT sandwiches or chicken tikka wraps, or a garage may get several cars with clutches to repair. Nobody has an explanation for this but it's a common experience in all walks of life. We even have a saying for it: 'Everything happens in threes,' and, sadly, this can be tragically true of major accidents.

Now you may think that, compared with the creation of the universe, counting brown shoes in a shopping mall is small beer, and you'd be right. Bear with me. There is more.

Perhaps Newton anticipated something of seriality, when he produced his law of universal gravitation. This states that every massive particle in the universe attracts every other massive particle with a force which is directly proportional to the product of their masses and inversely proportional to the square of the distance between them.[91] The effect of this law is observable in some natural science museums, where large iron balls suspended on wires are clearly being attracted toward one another. It's a form of clustering produced by gravity.

Following the work done by people like Kammerer and others, quantum physicists have now shown events in our universe tend to cluster into similar groups. Some have even labelled such particles 'love particles' and speak of' stickiness' and 'sensitivity'. Cosmologist Brian Swimme calls it 'allurement'.[92] On the cosmic scale it's how stars are born. In what we call space, uncountable quantities of hydrogen atoms float in a dark cloud and are gradually attracted together. As they become more and more tightly packed, they form a centre and begin to fuse with each other to form helium atoms. This releases their energy in terms of photons and heat. That's how a star is born. No one knows why this happens but everything depends on this 'seriality'; this 'allurement'.

In the world of psychology Jung coined the term 'synchronicity' to describe events with some common relevance which happen in clusters.

91 Wikipedia

92 The Universe is a Green Dragon, Brian Swimme, Bear & Company.

Someone reading a newspaper on a train sees the name 'Jenkins' in a newspaper article. He remembers he has a friend of that name and then hears the stranger next to him mention the name Jenkins in conversation. Often mundane and of no particular significance, synchronicities can also be life changing. A friend of mine got out of many life threatening situations during combat in the second world war simply because of series of remarkable coincidences. A fellow officer unexpectedly demanded his presence urgently and soon after he left his post a bomb exploded where he had been standing. He related numerous such stories to me, saying that his life was full of synchronicities. When we look back over the years, I'm sure we all see many clusters of seemingly unconnected events which contributed to significant outcomes. A multitude of intricately-related events took place almost simultaneously in Elizabeth's life and mine, that led to our meeting, buying a house, selling the house and moving to Herefordshire. In retrospect, it seemed as if an invisible hand was loading the dice to bring about fortuitous circumstances. Had I still been in my fundamentalist Christian mode, I would have put it all down to the direct intervention of a personal "God". Such 'synchronicity' Joseph Campbell defined as, 'All those miraculous coincidences which bring about the inevitable.'

But not all synchronous events are good. If I was delayed leaving home one morning and a driver lost control of a lorry which crashed into my car, that might be a series of negative synchronous events. Just by leaving the house on time, I might not have had the accident, though it might have happened to someone else. However, such a situation may equally well have generated a good outcome. A young man I know broke his leg and eventually married the radiographer who performed the X-ray.

Carl Jung showed that a person's attitude of mind can influence the outcomes of synchronous events. If I see a door of opportunity open and have the courage to go through it, then certain outcomes are almost inevitable. If my courage fails me, then I am likely to attract negative outcomes which take me along a different route. As I showed in Chapter Nine, this is the theme of the perennial hero in thousands of mythological stories arising out of cultures across the world. The hero begins the journey and meets someone who gives him a key. He then does something silly and loses the key and a spirit, perhaps appearing in human form, enables him to find the key again . . . and so on. Jung said those events we don't experience positively, we have to experience negatively. Perhaps that's why we describe some people as 'accident-prone'. Maybe they're just unlucky, because I know people who, although apparently very positive in their outlook, seem to attract a lot of bad luck. No doubt this is synchronicity too, but I've noticed their positive attitudes continually help them to bounce back.

The Greeks had a word for the kind of effect I've been trying to describe: *stokhastikos* or, in English, 'stochastic'. The word originally referred to the path of an arrow in flight. However good an archer you are, when you fire an arrow you only have a rough idea of which part of the target it's going to hit. Even though you may consistently hit the bull's-eye, you can never be sure on which part of the bull's-eye your arrow will land. If you're very unlucky, a sudden breeze may blow it off target altogether. Thus, the word 'stochastic' came to mean random but purposeful. Though scientists may not use this term, the condition is well established in quantum physics. Physicist Gerald L. Schroeder says,

> *'Quantum mechanics teaches that while the general path of a reaction may be predictable, the exact path is not. There is a probabilistic spread in the path that connects cause with effect.'*[93]

When you look at the history of evolution, you can't help but see a pattern of improvement as species have adapted better and better to their circumstances and the simple has evolved into the complex. Of course, some species, such as the dinosaurs, have been unable to adapt and others, crocodiles for instance, have hardly needed to change. But generally there has been a continuous improvement over millions of years. The outcome is a creature that could be conscious of its own consciousness: the Human

93 The Hidden Face of God, Gerald L. Schroeder, The Free Press.

Being. Indeed, many cosmologists now regard human consciousness as the universe being aware of itself.

For me, this stochastic principle demands a creation that arose, not from mechanical cause and effect, nor from the intervention of a supernatural power, but out of an intelligent 'enabling'. This 'enabling' does not sit outside of existence but is integral to it. However, this is a long way from what some have termed 'intelligent design'. The latter seems to be a watered-down version of the creationism I held to so dearly as a fundamentalist Christian. It was produced in America as a political expedient. The aim was to ensure something of creationism was taught in American schools alongside the principles of evolution. Intelligent design still demands a "God" entity who intervenes from outside the cosmos. Yet nature does not intervene, but patiently and kindly brings about changes 'organically' that will tend to be for the better.

There is another aspect of nature that appears to reveal the presence of what I call an 'enabling': intentionality. I realise that this word will drive friends of mine committed to materialism into a frenzy of denial, but I can only bear witness to what I observe. Far from being random or haphazard many of nature's inventions are, to my mind, intentional. I call as evidence the function of the *ductus arterios* in babies. As I understand it, before birth this function enables blood to bi-pass the baby's lungs. Until the moment of birth the baby's blood has been oxygenated by its mother because its own lungs have been full of liquid. At the moment of birth the *ductus arterios* shuts down and is subsequently absorbed into the body. This enables oxygen to get into the blood stream through the baby's lungs in the normal way. The timing of this event is critical. Too soon or too late and the baby will suffocate.

Surely this function had to be in place very early in the evolution of the human being and technically, it had to be functional *before* it was needed. Clearly, it is intended for a very specific purpose—to enable the baby to live in the womb. As soon as birth is triggered the *ductus arterios* stops operating and dies. How could any of this be accidental or random? How could it be the result of trial and error or a response to environmental pressures over a long period. It had to work first time or no baby could survive. It also had to be in place within one generation so it could be passed on to the next generation through DNA. What is this intelligence that enables conditions which anticipate a creature's future developmental needs—not on the odd occasion, but a million times after a million times?

I also call as evidence intentional adaptation (*somatic hypermutation)* which is a recent discovery by scientist John Cairns. He found that when bacteria are stressed, i.e. put into a potentially toxic solution, they produce an enzyme. This causes the bacteria to produce genes randomly. This they continue to do until they find a gene capable of overcoming their susceptibility to the toxicity. Then they replace the original gene with the new version and survive. Cairns proved organisms not only adapt to their environment but purposefully change their own genes. They can then pass on the adaptation to future generations.[94]

When a living organism randomly produces genes when stressed, and stops only when the right gene is found, it surely demonstrates purposeful activity. The organism appears to know what it's looking for since it does not replace its existing gene haphazardly but purposefully, and only when it has found the right one. Can it recognise what will work *before* the substitution takes place?

Science has shown us that creation is not the result of deliberate construction to a pre-determined design. That's how a human being would approach it. There was no blue print, no plan, no project with time-scales and costs, no bills of quantity. This discovery caused many to jump to the conclusion that there is no "God". However, some realised that maybe the conclusion should be that whatever we refer to as "God" isn't what we always imagined. This was certainly my response.

I prefer to think of creation as the result of a longing; a deep desire, which did not 'make' the bits and assemble them, but allured into being the conditions from which all things could emerge. What exists now is what *can* exist now. But the longing continues. The allurement never ceases. 'Love never fails.' What can be in a million years from now may be vastly

94 Spontaneous Evolution, p 150, Bruce H. Lipton and Steve Bhaerman, Hay House

different from anything we've known so far. Such a view, to my mind, recognises scientific knowledge *and* the intuition of the spiritual.

Although science may be a threat to fundamentalism, and quite rightly so, it is not a threat to spirituality. Indeed, scientific discoveries about how we have evolved into conscious beings informs and enhances my understanding of the spiritual. When I thought of "God" as a creator who planned and executed creation like an engineer, evolution couldn't make much sense. Now I think of 'God' as a non-coercive 'enabler' of what can be without force or coercion (that's the kind of "God" Jesus expresses in Matthew 5), it makes every sense, and explains billions of years of evolution.

Chapter Sixteen

"God" Revisited

It gradually dawned on me that the only thing I can know about whatever it is that I referred to as 'God', is that I can't know anything at all. Initially this gave me a problem. Like millions of others I had taken solace in an image of "God" as 'father'; one to whom I could talk to as a friend, like Father Brown in the series of books by that name. But I reached a point when that concept was no longer appropriate for me. I needed a "God" who was immanent as well as transcendent, a 'father' as well as an 'almighty', and without a coherent concept I felt as if I was floating rudderless in a sea of abstract thought. I could no longer think about 'God' as some kind of external person, so I needed to discover the immanence of the divine in a new way.

Bishop John Shelby Spong suggests we can only identify "God" from the evidence of the influences "God" has on our physical world. He uses the metaphor of Moses on the mountain. "God" would not permit Moses to see his face but let him catch a glimpse of his back (or according to some translations, his 'back side'!)[95]. The mystical message for me is that maybe all I can hope for in my search for 'God' is some evidence of where "God" has been. This may sound like a cop-out but there are many phenomena, the existence of which we can only know about from their effects. These include gravity, electricity, and weak and strong nuclear forces. Although we can measure each one of them and even harness them for our own use, we don't actually know what they are. We all experience and can measure their effects, yet we can't put these forces in a bottle or point to substances called 'gravity' or 'electricity'. I can't see them but I do experience them, all day and every day. So because we cannot point to a substance called "God" doesn't mean we don't benefit from the effect of 'Godness'. But this metaphor is very limited. What we refer to as "God" must surely be more than something like gravity.

95 Exodus 33:23

Although many of us don't like to admit it, we instinctively feel this 'isness', as Meister Eckhart called it. It seems to be more than simply one of the myriad natural forces that arose out of the Big Bang, yet to describe it as a person seems a gross devaluation. That's not to be critical of those who do, for in prescribing our religious doctrines we have actually been trying to understand the ineffable in the only way we could—by comparing it with what we know. With no evidence to the contrary, the best way our ancestors could find to express a notion of "God" was as a person. I don't think there's anything wrong in doing that still, provided we are aware of the limited view this expression of the ineffable gives. I must admit departing from my long and dearly held image of a 'him', who was a 'father', left me dangling for a while. Fortunately, there was a primordial urge within me to go on seeking for a deeper relationship with 'isness'.

The fact that, over hundreds of thousands of years, billions of people have felt a need arising within them to respond to a sense of the divine seems to confirm that there should be something to respond to. Some say this is simply a need for a sense of security. According to Matthew Alper it is a response to the realisation that we will die.[96] I agree that the realisation of death must have been a seminal moment in the evolution of human consciousness. Yet, as a species, we have learned to repress or displace that fear, not only through religious belief, but simply by not thinking about it. Most of us don't need religion to help us do that; our protective subconscious is quite capable of achieving this necessary deception with little or no help from the conscious mind. Mountain climbers, racing drivers and others involved in dangerous sports do it all the time—they have to, or they'd give up at the first sight of a threat. The ego-aware mind's ability at compartmentalisation and dissonant thinking is well-known.

Some argue that a gene is responsible for our religious inclinations; others suppose there is a 'god spot' in the brain that controls our behaviour. This may well be the case, but every physical feature in the human

96 The God Part of the Brain, Matthew Alper, Sourcebooks, Inc.

anatomy evolved as a response to something present outside the apparent external boundaries of the body. As Simone Weil says,

> *'Everything without exception which is of value in me comes from somewhere other than myself, not as a gift but as a loan which must be ceaselessly renewed.'*[97]

The eyes and visual cortex evolved to handle incoming photons of light; the digestive system to process incoming food; the lungs to handle the air I breathe, and bones and musculature to respond to gravity and the terrain. Our bodies have wonderfully adapted to the different environmental conditions they find themselves in. In deep jungles pygmy races evolved who could negotiate the entangled conditions easily, in mountainous areas those who could breathe thin air evolved, in hot countries people evolved with a pigmentation of skin that protected them from the damage from sunlight. If there is a "God" gene or a 'god spot' in the brain, what environmental condition did it evolve to meet? Beyond that which can currently be subjected to empirical study, is it possible there is a source of consciousness, intelligence and love that permeates all of creation? Might there be a source beyond what we think of as existent reality, beyond the duality of paired opposites? Could it be that to which we are instinctively responding? If so, when we speak of "God" we're not speaking of a person but of a personification.

The Non-Existent "God"

When I held a concept of "God" as some kind of person, He was invariably on the outside looking in. It follows that if "God" is an entity, then that god must be separate from the entity that is me. But then I awoke to realise that whatever it is I called "God" is not out there doing things to me in here, but is in here, right in the thick of it, seeking to do things out there. So if what we call "God" is not separate from me or any other entity, can such a "God" exist?

97 The Self, Simone Weil, from An Anthology, Modern Classics

The word 'exist' comes from the Latin '*exsistere*, where '*ex*' means 'out' and '*sistere'* means 'to stand'. In other words something that stands out or is separate from other things. It became clear to me "God" doesn't stand out or apart from anything. If someone yelled, 'Hey look, here comes God', the people in white coats would soon arrive in their black van. So, if "God" is integral to everything and cannot be understood as something separate, can it be said that "God" exists? The idea that "God" has no existence came as a quite shattering, though exciting experience. Theologian, Paul Tillich, expressed it like this:

> *'God does not exist. He is being itself beyond essence and existence. Therefore to argue that "God" exists is to deny him.'*[98]

And 9th century theologian John Scotus Eriugena said,

> *'We do not know what God is. God himself does not know what he is because he is not anything. Literally, God is not, for he transcends everything.'*[99]

I began to see to what extent it was true that God's being and my being are one, and therefore nothing exists separately. You don't get more immanent than that! The abstractions I found so difficult began to fade away. I became more deeply aware of just how close 'God' is—in Eastern thought 'closer than your breath'.

Enabler Rather than Creator

It became increasingly clear to me there isn't someone out there who 'ought to be doing something about' whatever turns out to be the current crisis. Rather, that there is within each one of us, what I shall call, for want of a better term, an 'enabling'. Rather than planning and manufacturing like some super-engineer, this 'enabling' is sensitive of opportunities to

98 Systematic Theology, Paul Tillich p. 307. The University of Chicago Press
99 Periphyseon, John Scottus Eriagena

'weight the dice' so that nature is able to fulfil, as completely as possible, what its environment and situation calls for.

I discovered that the word 'to create' didn't come into English until the 14th Century. It was derived from the word 'creature' and meant 'to grow or breed'. It didn't infer human inventiveness but natural growth. Thomas Aquinas said that if we get the creation wrong we get "God" wrong and to mistake "God" as an anthropomorphic inventor is a serious error. Understanding "God" as an Enabler, rather than Creator, radically changes our understanding of the development of the universe and the nature of suffering, and I will deal with the latter presently.

From the evidence I could gather, such an influence has been at the heart of evolution from the beginning of time. It is an understanding that can be found in many scriptures. The Taoist sage, Chuang Tzu, described heaven as *'that which acts on all and meddles with none.'* The Kena Upanishad expresses the relationship with the creator god, Brahman, beautifully:

> *'What cannot be spoken with words, but that whereby words are spoken: Know that alone to be Brahman, the spirit; and not what people here adore.*
> *What cannot be thought with the mind, but that whereby the mind can think: Know that alone to be Brahman, the spirit; and not what people here adore.*
> *What cannot be seen with the eye, but that whereby the eye can see: Know that alone to be Brahman, the spirit; and not what people here adore.*
> *What cannot be heard with the ear, but that whereby the ear can hear: Know that alone to be Brahman, the spirit; and not what people here adore.'*[100]

This is not a foreign concept to New Testament or Christianity, though I have to say the Christian scriptures seem to be ambivalent about it. Paul

100 Kena Upanishad, trans Juan Mascaró, Penguin Books

told the Colossians that in the Christ *'All things hold together'*. The Greek word means 'consist'. It is notable that Paul does not say that the Christ holds all things together. Quoting the Stoic philosopher, Epimenides, while preaching in Athens, Paul said of "God", *'In Him we live and move and have our being.'*[101] This contrasts starkly with Paul's teaching about Jesus returning from Heaven where he's been seated at the right hand of "God"[102]. Maybe it's an indication that such references shouldn't be taken as literally as my fundamentalist fellow believers and I had done.

What needs to be enabled for any given moment will depend on a multitude of factors. It may be the evolution of a particular biological function, finding a mate, achieving a successful hunt, making an escape to safety, producing a healthy birth or any one of a billion other events. What can be enabled is purely stochastic[103] and will be determined by many things, include pure chance. Sometimes an event can be enabled easily because all the conditions are right. Sometimes an event cannot be enabled at all because one essential element is missing or is of insufficient strength or quality. Often an event can be enabled but not to a very high standard. Let me try to explain this in practical terms:

Imagine two people of equal skill making bread. One has rather low grade flour, tap water, margarine and some dried yeast. The other has some high grade organic strong flour, spring water, olive oil and fresh yeast. Each makes a loaf, but the quality of the loaf which can be 'enabled' will depend on the quality of the materials used. However, the 'enabling' is exactly the same. That which we refer to as "God" always seeks to enable the best that can be for each one of us and all things.

As a fundamentalist Christian, the concept I had of "God" was of a being who would override nature. 'He' would, on a whim, impose 'His' will to produce a high grade loaf from low grade material. (This might be the interpretation of the story of Jesus turning water into wine, though I don't think that would be a correct understanding of the metaphor in the context of which it was told). Eventually I was able to consider the

101 Acts 17:28

102 Colossians 3:1

103 See page 169

evidence of my own eyes. With an open mind I observed what actually happens in evolution, in nature and in my day-by-day activities. The arguments for supernatural intervention fell away and I had to find a radically different way of thinking about "God".

Chapter Seventeen

The Nature of 'God'

A key difference between a 'creator' and an 'enabler' is that the creator is expected to overcome nature and force it to do what he wants, just as the Biblical "God" did in Exodus:

> *'Then the LORD said to Moses, See, I have made you like God to Pharaoh, and your brother Aaron will be your prophet. You are to say everything I command you, and your brother Aaron is to tell Pharaoh to let the Israelites go out of his country. But I will harden Pharaoh's heart, and though I multiply my signs and wonders in Egypt, he will not listen to you. Then I will lay my hand on Egypt and with mighty acts of judgement I will bring out my divisions, my people the Israelites. And the Egyptians will know that I am the LORD when I stretch out my hand against Egypt and bring the Israelites out of it.'*[104]

Poor old Pharaoh didn't stand a chance. Even if he had wanted to let the children of Israel go he couldn't, for "God" had hardened his heart, forcing him into a violent confrontation whether he liked it or not. This is not the "God" Jesus portrayed in Matthew 5 or that Paul described as love in 1 Corinthians 13. The "God" of Jesus is an enabler who 'does not resist (withstand) evil' and loves his enemy. If forced to go a mile, he goes two, gives to all who ask and never turns away a borrower (Matthew 5:38-42). The enabler is full of grace (unmerited favour) and grace doesn't work coercively because fundamental to it is the characteristic of non-violence. From this and simple observation of nature (see Chapter Fifteen), I conclude that that which we refer to as "God" is totally and utterly non-coercive and non-violent. "God" achieves nothing by the imposition of will. That's not to say when resistance or opposition is met, the 'enabler' rolls over and plays dead. If that was the case then nothing would be

104 Exodus 7:1-5

achieved. Rather the 'enabler' resists the wrong action non-violently and encourages the true action non-violently. This is the message of the *Tao Te Ching* and it accords beautifully with the Sermon on the Mount. The process I'm imagining might be rather like herding sheep with dogs. The sheep don't need to be bullied into going where they should be. All that needs to happen is to put a little resistance in the way they shouldn't go and a little encouragement in the way they should. The dog uses the nature of the sheep to control them. If you've ever watched sheep dog trials, you'll realise it's a bit of a hit and miss process, but most shepherds get their sheep home safely in the end. In the bigger picture, this is how evolution seems to have worked too. An obstacle here and another cleared there and nature just does what it ought to do under the circumstances.

In terms of human interaction this non-violent 'sheep-dog' principle can be illustrated by Gandhi's two-fold strategy of *Ahimsa* and *Satyagraha*. *Ahimsa* is enshrined in Jain, Hindu and Buddhist doctrine. It means respect for life, which is put into action by avoiding harm to any living thing. It is a doctrine of non-violence. Gandhi applied it in encouraging non-violent refusal to co-operate with bad government policies. The Sanskrit word, *Satyagraha*, means 'an insistent stating of the truth'. These were Gandhi's sheep dogs. With *Ahimsa*, he allowed and with *Satyagraha* he opposed—not by stating what was wrong, but in presenting what was true and right. With such tactics he liberated India.

Yet there was a third component in Gandhi's non-violent armoury—non-attachment, which is the subject of his favourite scripture, the *Bhagavad Gita* and one I covered in Chapter Fourteen. Without a highly developed sense of non-attachment, *Ahimsa* and *Satyagraha* would be almost impossible to implement. Indeed, during Gandhi's long struggle sometimes violence broke out. Not all of his supporters had learned the lessons of the *Bhagavad Gita* and the Sermon on the Mount. But the source of non-attachment is the enabling of which we are all outcomes. To find it we have first to recognise the source of attachment within us, the false self, then learn to rest in that perfection that is the Self. To understand the nature of that enabling within us, it will be useful to understand, in a little more depth, the nature of nature itself.

Evolution Enabled

We are all subject to the law of entropy—in other words we eventually run out of steam and come to an end. It is perfectly obvious that this happens to each individual life ineluctably, yet life has the ability to resist the effects of entropy for quite a long time. It has found a way to utilize ever increasing amounts of energy to evolve ever increasing levels of complexity and thus defer the ultimate entropic outcome long enough to reproduce itself and start over. As Rumi says, '*Out of one huge NO comes a chorus of yeses.*'[105] Plants are nurtured by the earth and climate, animals and insects are nurtured through plants and each other. Mothers suckle and protect their young and so 'generation succeeds to generation'.

Some biologists call this 'kin selection'. They say that the only motivation behind helping a fellow being arises out of the desire to protect and promote the genes they have in common. They also suggest this evolved into what they call 'reciprocal altruism': doing a favour for someone whom we hope will some day return it. This is a perfectly rational, if highly mechanistic, way of looking at nature. It doesn't, however, explain the level of altruism where people give their own lives to save a perfect stranger. How is that reciprocal? Reciprocal altruism also ignores the fact that our brains are equipped with mirror neurons which enable us to enter into an empathic relationship with others. In other words, to feel another's pain and respond as if it were our own pain. Thousands of experiments with animals and humans, both baby and adult, have proved without doubt that we are hardwired for empathy—not merely evolved to keep account of the favours we give and receive.

In human experience nurturing has a lot more to it than just an instinct-driven response, though undoubtedly there's something of that at its root. I see a vital principle at work: *It is in the nature of nature to nurture.*

---

105 'Soul Houses', Rumi, from Bridge to the Soul, Coleman Barks, Harpur Collins.

In the human context, we call this love. All of us, biologists included, prefer to understand our own relationships in terms of love rather than 'kin selection' or 'reciprocal altruism'. I can't imagine a biologist at his wedding ceremony insisting on using the form of words, 'I promise to reciprocate altruistically'!

Enabling Love

If nurture is love then love is the very basis of life, the nature of the earth and the nature of that which enables the earth. So, rather than using the term "God", which has become so tainted by history and misunderstanding, I've begun to use the term 'Enabling Love'. This doesn't describe a being or entity, which has existence as we have existence, but an intelligent, compassionate and non-violent, non-coercive influence at the heart of the universe. This is not a father, although embodied in fatherhood; not a mother, although embodied in motherhood. Enabling Love describes a relationship rather than a person; a phenomenon rather than an entity.

Intelligent design and creationism describe a quite different kind of 'God'. What they describe is metaphorically like fuel in the engine whereas 'Enabling Love' is like oil. Fuel forces the pistons up and down and drives the machine along but, without the oil, the engine would seize up within minutes. Oil keeps all the working parts in a good relationship with one another so that friction and wear are minimal. In my metaphor the fuel is not an almighty "God" figure but more like the pervasive energy of the 'Big Bang'. It courses through every particle, every wave form and every being every second of every day. Yet maybe it's even more than that. Maybe it's that which caused the big bang in the first place. Even so, 'Enabling love' is now the universe's lubricant. It facilitates the relationship of the particles and the entities which arise from those particles. It seems to inhabit the spaces between, just as oil does. My oil metaphor is imperfect, as all metaphors are, but it's the nearest I can get to expressing what I believe I can observe in the natural world and the cosmos from which it arose.

In my early days as a Fundamentalist Christian, I received a lot of comfort from holding the concept of a personal "God" who intervenes. Yet this notion of "God", even then, generated more problems for me than it solved. It left many questions unanswered: Why is there evil in the world? Why do the innocent suffer? Why doesn't "God" always intervene? What criteria does He use? I could find answers, certainly, but all the answers were really excuses and left a deep root of dissatisfaction in me. The view I've just outlined solves for me just about all the problems I've had with "God".

From the evidence available, other than the supposition that the Bible should be taken literally, the universe as we know it didn't arise from the imposition of divine will. It didn't come into being as a coercive act which altered the nature of things. Neither can it be said to have arisen out of totally random events, though randomness is obviously involved. Rather, it seems to have arisen out of what I can only describe as a desire, a longing that sometimes had to wait millions of years before all the right components came together in the right place and in the right proportions and relationships. And this desire, this longing is not for some specific form, but for outcomes of which form is merely the vehicle of delivery. Unlike the creator "God" of the Bible, the 'Enabling Love' of the observable universe does not intervene to short-circuit nature but where a way to change a situation for the positive *within* nature can be found, 'Enabling Love' will find it. If I can recover from having a cancerous illness, then the components of that recovery will be inclined to congregate. If not, then I will die, but that's OK because death isn't the worst thing that can happen to me. In this scenario there seems to be no need for a great divine plan. No need for one who sits outside of creation, tinkering with it like a clockmaker. The imposition of a divine plan would necessitate coercion, often by violence, to force things into submission. 'Enabling love' is totally non-violent and non-coercive, so there is no timetable, no plan; perhaps there is just a desire and a longing for the best that can be. How non-human!

Man has always needed to justify his own violence. That is why this totally non-violent aspect of the divine has been largely hidden from us for generations. Once the Christian church got into bed with the state, in the fourth century, it could no longer promote non-violence. It became even more necessary to think of "God" as a forceful male than the totally non-violent and loving enabler Jesus spoke of. Being a partner in power with any state makes it essential to reject non-violence as a basis for living and this filters down to the whole society, a whole culture. Very soon the church was using violence itself to exterminate opposition to its view of orthodoxy. When a war begins, the clergy bless, not only the troops but their armaments. And everyone, even the non-religious, say 'Amen'.

The Nature of Love

Paul's definition of love in 1 Corinthians helped me to understand a little more about this non-violent enabler. Paul's beautiful poem is worth learning by heart:

'Love is patient, Love is kind.
It does not envy,
It does not boast.
It is not proud.
It is not self-seeking.
It is not easily angered.
It keeps no record of wrong.
Love does not delight in evil
But rejoices with the truth.
It always protects, always trusts;
Always hopes, always perseveres. Love never fails.'

When I first understood that these qualities pervade the universe, I felt full of gratitude. I began to realise that what I had always thought of as a creative process, with "God" as the initiator, was actually a 'co-creative' process. It's about co-operation, not imposition. It's as if 'Enabling Love' chooses to be limited by what is possible in the physical universe and this, I believe, is non-violence at work, the heart of Jesus' message, epitomised in his life, his suffering and his death.

Lao Tzu said that '*Serenity and peace are the norm of the earth.*' Despite the evidence of violent confrontations between creatures, the principles of non-violence demonstrated by Jesus nevertheless seem to be the main way in which nature works. Acts of gratuitous and malicious violence are rare in the animal kingdom and, when violence does occur, it doesn't last long. True, many animals use violence to hunt, but it is not gratuitous or malicious. When predators are not hunting they can go quite near prey animals without provoking much more than curiosity. Hunting out of sheer greed is extremely rare. As I suggested earlier, prey creatures have tended overwhelmingly to evolve defensive faculties, rather than attacking ones. They're equipped better to run away than to stand and fight. Camouflage, prickles, smells and armour are common. Horns are common too, but they are used to protect the young and demonstrate fecundity more often than they are used to attack others with malice—even enemies. The evolutionary response of prey animals is for herding and flight. If they had the wit, they might, as a herd, run down a predator and trample it to death—a not unknown phenomenon—but nature rarely provokes that strategy.

So whereas I'm not claiming a romanticised passivity on the part of nature, I am suggesting it is not as 'bloody in tooth and claw' as Lord Tennyson would have us believe. Man may provide an exception to this. However, simple observation of day-to-day behaviour quickly shows that we are more co-operative than competitive. Indeed, violent behaviour among humans has been shown to be declining in almost all societies world-wide[106]. We get the idea that it's far more prevalent than it is from our news-media, which trade on the brain's predilection for finding anomalies. This instinct has evolved for the purpose of self-preservation, but our news-media easily stimulate it by producing a preponderance of negative news. Look around you. Most people are doing good things to

106 The Better Angels of our Nature, Stephen Pinker, Allen Lane

most other people most of the time. As Erasmus pointed out in the 16th century, as a species we are not equipped for war. We have no horns or antlers, no sabre teeth or claws to tear. We have no thick hides or thick fur, we're not very strong and can't run very fast. No, says Erasmus, we're not equipped for war, we're equipped for love.[107] To commit the atrocity of war we have to make tools to overcome the limitations with which nature endowed us!

If such non-violence and non-resistance has evolved in the natural world, might this say something about the character of the 'Enabler'? What if that which we refer to as "God" refuses to impose 'His' will to dominate the creation? What if this enabler sees the principle of non-violent non-resistance as the best way to nurture nature? This radically changes my understanding of "God" *and* the problem of suffering. (It also blows most of Paul's theology right out of the water! Sorry about the violent metaphor!)

This 'self-imposed' limitation on the part of the Enabler is expressed in Taoism as the principal of 'wu wei' or non-ado. The Tao Teh Ching expresses the way in which I suggest 'Enabling Love' operates, like this:

'The Tao is always at ease.
It overcomes without competing,
Answers without speaking a word,
Arrives without being summoned,
Accomplishes without a plan.
Its net covers the whole universe,
And although its meshes are wide,
It doesn't let a thing slip through.'[108]

'Enabling Love' is far removed from Yahweh of the pillar of smoke and pillar of fire; It is far from the one who flooded the earth, destroyed Sodom and Gomorrah, sent plagues on the Egyptians and demolished the

107 Against War, Desiderius Erasmus, Edited by Lewis Einstein, The Merrymount Press, 1907
108 Tao Teh Ching 73 Trans: Stephen Mitchell

walls of Jericho. ‘Enabling Love’ would not, could not, do this. And if it follows the principles of non-resistance faithfully, neither could it impose strict laws of conduct on people. Why, it wouldn't even punish their disobedience! But then, you may ask, without the law what's to stop us from misbehaving?

When I look around at the chaos generated by humanity, I observe that religion and law have had little restraint on human misbehaviour. On the other hand, it is observable throughout society that love, more often than not, restrains bad behaviour and promotes good. It is generally the children of abusive homes that are themselves abusive. Richard Rohr says he never met a man in prison for murder who had had a good relationship with his father—if he'd ever known who his father was. When we love children and treat them justly and fairly, they normally grow up to be loving, just and fair. It is perfectly clear, though many wish to deny it, that our punitive justice system emphatically does not work. The expanding prison population and the levels of recidivism prove this without a doubt: around half of all offenders return to prison for a second offence. Though I don't suggest wrongdoers shouldn’t be punished, I do question the methods we use, for these are only driving most offenders deeper into a state of 'unlovingness'. So, without the law, what is there to stop us from misbehaving? The answer is simply love. (If you want to have clear evidence for this then do see the film, ‘Doing Time, Doing Vipassana’ on YouTube.)

As I've grown in my experience of and relationship with ‘Enabling Love’, I've found an increased desire to act compassionately. Learning about non-attachment helped considerably in this. My experience as a fundamentalist Christian was of life as a battleground, where the devil, as a ravening lion, was on the prowl, constantly trying to devour me. Now I'm freed from the fear of offending 'The Almighty', I can more fully experience the embrace of non-violent love, which comes to me from the very core of the universe itself.

Chapter Eighteen

The Mess We're In

As a Christian I had it all worked out: since Adam, all had sinned—that was my answer to why we're in the mess we're in. There was only one way to get out of it and that was to believe in Jesus Christ as your personal saviour. When you did that everything in the garden was rosy. Your sins were forgiven and you had a guarantee that Jesus would one day whisk you out of the mess, so you could live happily ever after with him in heaven or on a renewed earth.

As for the mess, well that would continue, at least until after the Judgement. But the more I examined this concept, the less appealing it became. My simplistic views raised the problem of what "God" would do about the 99% of all humans who had ever lived and who would never hear the gospel—not the one I was preaching anyway. This might include babies who died and those whose parents had kept them from hearing the gospel—and what about really good people who believed differently from me? Was "God" really going to make them burn in hell for eternity when they nevertheless demonstrated the fruits of the spirit in their lives? Most of those I worshipped with avoided such issues, bundling them into the skeleton cupboard along with other annoying questions.

But one thing is clear, the world really is in a mess and we now have the numbers to prove it. It's a catalogue of inequality, misery and desolation resulting from greed and selfishness. Although the figures will have changed by the time this book reaches publication, sadly, they are likely to become worse rather than better. So here is a brief overview of the mess we're in:

- 6% of people possess 59% of the world's wealth
- 80% of the world's population live in poverty
- 70% are illiterate
- 50% suffer from hunger and malnutrition
- 1% own a computer

- 1% have a university degree
- 500 million people are suffering war, prison, torture or are close to death from starvation.
- 3 billion people are threatened with violence because of their religion.
- Estimates of the number of people who are enslaved range from about 10 million to 30 million, according to policy makers, activists, journalists and scholars. Other studies in 2006 put the range between 24 million and 32 million.
- Some 16,000 species are known to be threatened with extinction.
- Only 1.9 million species have been described out of an estimated 5–30 million species which exist.
  In the last 500 years, human activity has forced 844 species to extinction (or extinction in the wild).
- One in every four mammals and one in every eight birds is facing a high risk of extinction in the near future.
- One in three amphibians and almost half of all tortoises and freshwater turtles are threatened.
- The current species extinction rate is estimated to exceed the natural or background' rate by 100 to a 1,000 times.
- Of the 129 recorded bird extinctions, 103 are known to have occurred since 1800, indicating an extinction rate 50 times the background rate.
  The total number of threatened animal species has increased from 5,205 to 7,266 since 1996.
- Habitat loss and degradation affect 86% of all threatened birds, 86% of mammals and 88% of threatened amphibians.
- All 21 species of albatross are now under threat globally, compared to only three in 1996, as a result of long-line fishing. Such fishing threatens 83 species of bird. [109]

109 www.iucnredlist.org

A Very Short History of Violence

Human beings have always had a violent streak. Some think this is a genetically inherited tendency obtained from the ancestor we share jointly with the Chimpanzee. Along with chimpanzees we are one of the few apes that deliberately commit infanticide and genocide. Even so, chimpanzees spend most of their time browsing, mating, sleeping and playing. Only occasionally does violence, and especially homicidal violence, break out. Studies have shown that only .036% (1 in 10,000) chimpanzees die from warfare-like violence. Figures for human communities vary and are, on very rare occasions, higher than this but usually much lower.[110] We are also closely related to the Bonobo, which evolved at the same time as the Chimpanzee but on the other side of, what was for them, the impassable Congo river. The bonobo's answer to any crisis is sex—they make love, not war. I guess we've inherited something of that too.

Among the remains of early homo sapiens there is certainly evidence of violence between individuals and small groups. But organized violence, in the form of warfare, is a relatively new phenomenon. Archaeologists have shown that defensive structures, such as hill forts are a recent innovation. For thousands of years, communities of people lived with little or no inter-community violence. They didn't need to build defensive structures or develop the machinery of war. The skeletons in primitive prehistoric tombs attest to this. Very few of their owners died violently. Working in the Balkans, world-renowned archaeologist Marija Gimbutas discovered the remains of Neolithic societies who had, apparently, lived without warfare for 1500 years. So although violence has been a dominant aspect of world cultures for some 6000 years, we should not consider that it is an essential aspect of human make-up. None of us want war and we label negatively as 'warmongers' those who try to activate it.

With the rise of warrior communities and the consequent change from matriarchal to patriarchal societies, violent tendencies in human societies began to positively ferment. This change seems to have happened gradually in the early Bronze Age, or perhaps the late Neolithic, when the

110 http://en.wikipedia.org/wiki/List_of_wars_and_anthropogenic_disasters_by_death_toll

concept of ownership of land had become widely established. In the beginning of this era violence was usually sporadic and arose largely between one city state and another. We find evidence for this in both the Iliad and the Bible. Warfare was possibly a scaled-up version of the periodic skirmishes that took place between hunter-gatherers over territory. But a sudden, and largely unexplained, collapse of Bronze Age societies plunged the world into a dark age nearly 2000 years before the 'Dark Ages'.

It seems to have begun with the hydraulic societies which achieved such success in the Middle East, among them Ur of the Chaldees, Abraham's home town. Unwittingly, their irrigation canals caused water to evaporate more quickly than in rivers, and the relative lack of current also meant that water soaked away. Evaporation concentrated salts and as the water soaked into the earth it slowly poisoned the soil.[111] There is now evidence that crop production in the middle east was in decline over a long period. Could this be why Abraham took his fateful journey? Steve Taylor cites the migration of Saharasians, in particular Indo-European communities during the 4th millennium BCE. This resulted from deserts creeping farther north as a result of climate change, driving people to find new territories. But these people had developed a much more egotistical approach to life and were quite prepared to take land by bloody violence, an almost unheard of event in the lives of the defenceless Neolithic communities.[112]

Populations had increased considerably early in the Bronze Age and this resulted in the 'goddess' societies, and their egalitarian influence, being repressed by the increasing male domination in warrior communities. By the early Iron Age a new breed of leadership had been established, as the culture of Saharasian communities spread across the world. It brought humanity into an era in which, rather than agriculture or commerce, warfare became the chosen means of survival. With their own lands unable to support the population, the strategy for survival became one of

111 The Empathetic Civilisation, p221, Jeremy Rifkin, Tarcher Penguin
112 The Fall, Steve Taylor, iFF Books

stealing from the neighbours. A similar strategy occurred in the north when Vikings raided Britain.

Instead of skirmishes between tribes over territory or possessions (the possession of Helen of Troy for example) there arose, in about the eighth century BCE, a thirst for wider territorial conquest. Among the first warrior kings who led this revolution was Sennacherib of the Assyrians. To the Assyrians warfare was not just a response to a threat but a policy of state, the sole aim of which was to expand territory at any cost! This war culture seems to have become so deeply embedded in the collective ego world-wide that it has blighted the lives of every generation of every nation, directly or indirectly to the present day. It was from this event and subsequent upheavals, recorded in the books of 2 Kings, 2 Chronicles and Isaiah, that the Old Testament took form.

One of the signs of a violent society is the way they label their enemies. Jews labelled non-Jews as 'gentiles'. Europeans labelled Muslims as 'Saracens' during the Crusades and denounced them all as evil-doers. Saxons labelled the British tribes the 'Welsh' (outsiders). Early Christians labelled Romans as 'Pagans'—nature worshippers. Some Muslims label those who do not believe as they do '*kafirs*'. Christians and Muslims have labelled those who don't believe as they do, 'infidels'. Nazis labelled Jews 'mice', 'rats' and 'swine'. Soldiers of the Allied Nations labelled Germans, '*krauts*' - cabbages. The Japanese labelled the Americans and British '*kichiku eibei*', demons.

Labelling makes the object of the label less than human and therefore fair game. This is a perverted action of the ego, the job of which is to define and differentiate. The 'false self' is devious. It can always excuse violence, even though it knows in its heart of hearts (the influence of the Self) that violence is wrong. For instance, European Christians managed to go along with the obscenity of slavery for several hundred years, and politicians have always been able to resort to war, often labelling it as 'defence'. Only one condition is at the root of all this chaos—a human culture which arises among a people who have not recognised or overcome the influences of the ego's false self.

Is There a Solution?

I once expressed to a friend, rather eloquently I thought at the time, my alarm about humanity's headlong rush for disaster. I said, 'I can't see how a ship of six billion souls can avoid running into an iceberg of its own creation.'

He replied that I was using the wrong metaphor. 'Human beings aren't boiler-plated together like a great ship,' he said. 'Rather, they're like fishes in a shoal. Each fish is able to influence only six others in its immediate vicinity, yet that's all it takes to make the great shoal move like a single organism.'

This made me realise whole societies and cultures are capable of making rapid changes in the way they think and behave. I thought about some of the radical changes of attitudes in my own lifetime toward women's rights, homosexuality, animal rights, health and safety, environmental issues and smoking, to name but a few. Maybe disaster isn't inevitable after all.

As I reflected on this over the subsequent months I became aware of how great movements in recent history have wrought far-reaching changes among millions of people with minimal or no violence. Unlike changes engendered by warfare, changes brought about non-violently take many years. Despite the fact that progress is sometimes slight and the best that can be enabled is sometimes mediocre, change is nonetheless 'purposefully' achieved. It is limited by the ego, both collective and individual. I cite as evidence for this assertion that since 1945 many remarkable non-violent 'enablings' have entered the historical record.

- In 1948 Gandhi and his people recovered, by largely non-violent means,[113] delivered India from the oppression of British rule.
- Since the 60s, acts of non-violent civil disobedience by black Americans, like those of Rosa Parks and such visionaries as Dr. Martin Luther King, have brought civil rights to millions of

113 See also Chapter 17

oppressed Black Americans. (Sadly, that nation still has some way to go as recent events have shown)

- The 'velvet revolution' in Czechoslovakia freed the country from oppression in 1989.
- In the same year Poland was freed from Communism by the persistent non-violent efforts of *Solidarity* led by Lech Walensa.
- Also in 1989 we saw the miracle of the fall of the Berlin Wall.
- Led by Nelson Mandela, long imprisoned for his non-violent opposition, black South Africans were freed from the evils of apartheid, largely by non-violent means, in 1994.
- In 1998, the bloody violence of Northern Ireland was brought to an end by non-violent means, largely through the work of John Hulme. People, tired of the futility of violence, enabled shared rule of that troubled province.
- In 2010, thanks to international and internal pressure, Aung San Suu Kiy, began to lead Burma on its journey back to democratic rule, again without violence. (It is very sad that she has not followed through this good start and has subsequently failed many of her people and disgraced herself in the eyes of the world.)

Reports have indicated that some commentators feel that even the war leaders are beginning to realise that, if they had done more to help develop standards of living in Afghanistan and Iraq in the past, they would not feel the need to be resorting to violence to the same extent now. Belatedly, some humanitarian development in these countries is getting a higher priority from governments and its fruits are being seen in peaceful co-operation.

In 2011 non-violent protests began to break out all over the middle east. We called it the Arab Spring, but sadly, the response of some governments has been militantly aggressive and those who began their protests peacefully have been drawn into armed conflict. Non-violence is a difficult principle to learn after a five-thousand year history of war. It is notable that, whereas the death toll in those countries in which a non-violent opposition has been used usually runs into hundreds, the death toll in those countries where violent opposition occurs runs into thousands.

Modern analytical and research techniques have identified a strange phenomenon. Although to people of the 21st Century it may appear that the world is becoming a more violent place, in fact the reverse is true. Casualties of war and the number of murders have increased, but not as a percentage of the population. That has declined. So the reason for more violence is because there are simply more of us. The actual proportion of people committing violence in practically all societies is becoming smaller.[114] This gives me hope.

Is it possible that the 21st century will see nations unite to remove the cause of war from the human heart? Unless we do, we face awful traumas as populations exceed resources in many lands. Maybe we have, as many suspect, gone beyond the point where the situation can be retrieved but it's not in the nature of nature to give up. Like John Cairns' bacteria, life will seek to maintain itself and overcome the toxicity which threatens it.

What Can We Do?

At the top of my list is that we must each find the courage to take responsibility for our own deviant egos. As adults we need to recognise the action of the ego's 'false self' and teach our children to recognise it too. Understanding why we behave as we do is the first step to taking control over how we behave. In recognising a problem we are half way to solving it. For those who, like me, are minded towards spirituality, this amounts to an understanding of the Self and its importance in our understanding of the self. For those not inclined toward the spiritual approach, a basic understanding of the development of the brain, the persona and the operation of consciousness may be effective. But in all this we need to recognise the potential of non-violent action for solving all human problems. Only by detaching ourselves from the negative influences of the ego's false self can non-violence become effective.

114 The Better Angels of Our Nature, Stephen Pinker, Allen Lane

Schools will need to play a major rôle in this 'velvet revolution'. Although our generation may build on work done by the visionaries of peace from previous generations, we have a long journey before us. It is the next generation and the generations after that which will need to nurture the seeds sown and bring them into maturity. Current restrictions on national curricula and the imposition of politically-driven educational policies have more to do with maintaining capitalism and consumerism than delivering education. As teachers free themselves from these restrictions, there may be increasing opportunities to develop more supportive cultures. Opportunities may arise to introduce peace studies into the curriculum more widely. Already the practice of mindfulness is being widely introduced into schools and this is a major step towards releasing ourselves from the domination of the ego-self. We build on this with initiatives to help pupils understand how to handle those arch-enemies of the human psyche, fear and desire. As each fish influences six others, we can move together as one body towards a future where peace, love and joy really do prevail.

But What of Religion?

Does religion have any rôle to play in all this? I believe it could have, provided it undergoes some radical changes. The rôle of religion should be to bring each of its followers to maturity. Every mature follower should be capable of living independently of the ‘mother’ in order to realise his or her own expression of spirituality. In this, religion has largely failed, and this failure is especially true of the Abrahamic faiths: Judaism, Christianity and Islam. Religion, as we know it, provides care and nurture for spiritual infants. Sadly, leaders often continue in their rôle of changing nappies and keeping toddlers on reins. Consequently their spiritual children never grow up into fully mature spiritual adults. We find among the religious, a widespread dependency culture which is often encouraged by pastors, priests, rabbis and imams. Followers are kept on the reins of doctrine because otherwise, deprived of the mature faculty of discernment, they would wander out into the traffic of heresy or, "God" forbid, into someone else's religious garden. They are told that, without religion, they are weak and unable to cope with the world and therefore they *are* weak and need to be constantly cleaned up by their carers. This experience simply reinforces thoughts of inadequacy and they continue on a spiritual path that describes a circle. Followers simply trudge along a clearly defined track round and around the base of the mountain, instead of launching themselves upward to the peak where all is one. Religion, then is simply a collective 'false self' which overlays the 'True Self' with "many hides", as Eckhart put it, but in the form of doctrine.

Leaders may imagine that if people begin to think independently the church will fall apart. Yet this isn't necessarily so. As in my own experience, along with spiritual maturity comes a greater acceptance of others 'as they are'. Just as it is the 'soul' of individuals that is their reality, and not their form, so it is for organisations. Religion is only the form which contains the 'soul'. The 'collective soul', the 'True Self', always seeks unity. It is the collective ego's 'false self'—religious or not—which seeks division.

Large numbers of religious leaders have to awaken to an understanding of their rôle as bringing their people to spiritual maturity and therefore to unity, so they are no longer dependent on doctrine and the 'mother' establishment. I feel many people today pay lip service to this ideal. Sadly, many leaders are not spiritually mature in themselves and so are incapable of leading others into spiritual maturity. I can't help someone to a higher place on the mountain than where I myself stand.

Some fear enlightened persons will forsake the establishment which brought them to maturity, and maybe this is a price they have to pay. It is the individual's spiritual life that is important, not bums on seats, nor even the establishment's survival. It is cruel that so many people's spiritual development is stifled by their religious establishment. Simone Weil argues well that only individuals may have opinions, not groups. She says:

> *'. . . when a group starts having opinions, it inevitably tends to impose them on its members. Sooner or later these individuals*

find themselves debarred . . . from expressing opinions opposed to the group, unless they care to leave it.' [115]

But enlightened members of the congregation can be valuable carers in their own right, helping others to find their own pathway into mature spiritual experience, not through coercive adherence to doctrine and dogma,
but through a loving relationship with the 'True Self'. It will take much humility to enable such a radical change to happen.

From my own experience, I would say that dependency on doctrine is the greatest threat to spiritual maturity. In the epistles to Timothy and Titus, the writer had much to say about 'sound doctrine', though he never spelled out precisely what he meant by the term. It is important to remember he was dealing with a 'baby' church and so doctrine was going to be essential until the new Christians had a mature experience of 'God'. To the Corinthians Paul wrote, 'When I was a child, I talked like a child, I thought like a child, I reasoned like a child. When I became a man, I put the ways of childhood behind me.' It is in this passage Paul also speaks of knowing only in part and trusting the power of love. What happens when you mature spiritually as an adult is that you lose the need for someone to tell you 'do this' or 'don't do that'. You no longer need to have your doctrine on paper because it's written in your heart, yet not in concepts but in the principle of love. It is no longer something you merely know about, but something you experience and that colours everything you think and do. The writers of the Upanishads said that, to the truly enlightened person, the scriptures are like a well in a flooded land.

I am constantly amazed at the degree of common understanding there is among those who have matured spiritually. In recent years I've met with Anglicans, Catholics, United Reformers, Unitarians, Evangelicals, Quakers, Buddhists, Pagans, Theosophists, Sufis and many others. Within each one of them I found a true heart of spiritual love. If we had met on the

115 Simone Weil—An Anthology, p128, Modern Classics

basis of doctrine we could never have got close. But at every meeting we each recognised in the other the 'light that lightens every man'.

It's important to remember that, like all spiritual truth, doctrine never points to itself, it always points beyond itself. The Pharisees of Jesus' day were brilliant at doctrine and Jesus called them hypocrites and 'whited sepulchres'. Spiritually, they were still toddlers. I've discovered that, once I entered a living experience of 'God', I didn't need doctrine to keep me on the straight and narrow. Why, I didn't even need to speak of "God". My surrender to 'Enabling Love' is sufficient. As a result of this I don't stop reading scriptures and inspirational literature but my reading and understanding is so much more satisfying than ever it could be by seeing only through the lens of my religion.

That doesn't mean to say all opinions about reality are equally true or equally valid. The reasons I give for my experiences may be considerably different from the reasons my religious and spiritual friends give for the same kind of experience in their own lives. The reasons are not important —that is form. It's the experience that counts —that is soul. So that which holds the various belief systems together is not having a common doctrine. It's not even having some aspect of doctrine in common, as the ecumenical movement might have it. It's about common experience, and that will invariably bring a common focus to our relationship with our universe, our natural world and other people. Within these three elements of common focus will be an experience of whatever it is we refer to as 'God'.

The Future of Religion

Looking at the trajectory of religion in the West, I strongly suspect that there will be some major changes in the next generation. The rest of the world will probably get to this point too in a few generations. It is summed up in a few words by three spiritual leaders I greatly admire, Joseph Campbell, Eckhart Tolle and Russel Williams. I leave you with their words:

'. . . we are at this moment participating in one of the very greatest leaps of the human spirit to a knowledge not only of our outside nature but also of our own deep inward mystery.'
Joseph Campbell

'What is arising now is not a new belief system, a new religion, spiritual ideology, or mythology. We are coming to the end not only of mythologies but also of ideologies and belief systems.'
Eckhart Tolle

'We've reached a point now where we are moving on to the next stage. This is why the world is in such a troubled state at the moment. It's preparing for the end of one phase and the beginning of a new, which will quietly overlap. Throughout the past, civilizations have died and new phases have begun. This is the point we are at now. I don't know precisely what is going to happen next but I am well aware that we're reaching the end of our civilization. But it doesn't mean to say the end of the world—nobody said that. The world is moving so fast now that it has to come to some sort of an end, and then start up again. In the process, the human race will begin to change emotionally and mentally so as to be able to appreciate the spirit far more than the physical. That will become so much easier. We are certainly at a momentous point in history.'
Russel Williams

Postscript

As a fundamentalist Christian I had certainty. It was very comforting but it was an illusion. Faith is not belief in the unbelievable, neither is it blind. Faith is about trust. Trust in that which enables all things to be, trust that such an enabling is always motivated by love and that, ultimately, nothing can happen, good or bad, that isn't right. I find myself happily blending in with spiritual people from all faiths and those from none. I have learned to recognise 'the master's voice' and to discern something of the reality behind the form, which we call 'truth'. Where I go from here I have no idea but I know the path will form under my feet as I move forward. I hope that in sharing these thoughts you may be enabled to take your own next step into the void and feel secure. That's what faith is.

Appendix

Activities to Help Develop Spiritual Experience

Your ego's false sense of self is the source of practically all your problems. In both its individual and collective form the ego is the source of all the world's evils. In order to have any power over people the ego must remain hidden. As long as we are unconscious of its control over us we remain prisoners in our own bodies. In recognising that the ego is the source of the inappropriate fears and desires that assail you day after day and in becoming aware of how these manifest in you, is to remove its defences and expose its weaknesses. However, this is not to disarm the ego. That is something you cannot do; you certainly can't achieve that by will power. To try to overcome the ego with will power is to try to overcome the ego with the ego. That's like having a one-armed wrestling match—against yourself! If you win you lose.

The ego cannot overcome the ego but you have within yourself a source that can. To find this source requires an approach that is exactly the opposite of the one your ego-self would take. Your ego-self seeks to control and will tend to use force to achieve that if need be. When it cannot control it makes you feel frustrated and angry, and when that doesn't achieve anything it may make you either violent or depressed. The ego is fuelled by emotion and is constantly looking for activities or things that will make you feel good to distract you from a permanent underlying sense of dissatisfaction. If you want to test whether this is so, how long can you sit comfortably in a waiting room without anything to do?

Your ego-awareness with its underlying sense of dissatisfaction has developed over your lifetime aided unconsciously by input from parents, siblings, relations, peers, teachers, colleagues and everything that life throws at you. It's been a lifetime habit and it isn't going to go away with one wave of a magic wand. But neither is it going to go away as the result of a wrestling match—no matter how strong you are.

The solution is something that your ego-self is probably not at all comfortable with: silence. This is a great mystery. To overcome the powerful influence of your ego—to bring it to rest—you must do nothing, and by 'nothing' I mean exactly that. Have no expectations, no plans, make no effort to achieve a particular state of consciousness, hold no beliefs. Simply find a quiet place where you will not be disturbed. Sit upright with an open body position (legs uncrossed, unless you are on a cushion on the floor; arms unfolded, hands resting in your lap. Simply be comfortable. Don't assume a particular posture with the idea that it is necessarily 'spiritual'. Then simply be aware of your breath. Allow your mind to let go of any thoughts that pervade it and turn your awareness on how you feel in the environment in which you are. Just notice without comment. I call it 'knowticing'. Thought will keep trying to take over your mind and, when this happens, just turn your attention back on to your breath.

The Tao Te Ching says that the mind is like a muddy pool, which if left still for long enough will become clear. The mud sinks to be bottom. We do not become still by trying hard, we become still by doing nothing. If you can be open enough and silent enough and still enough for long enough, something wonderful happens. Your ego-self, whom you have always thought you are, becomes still and you sense-feel a presence that is at peace with itself and with everything else. This is the True Self that seems to be the very source of your being. Once you become acquainted with this Self, and know how to find it, you begin to recognise it in others. Then you know that this is not *your* True Self but the True Self of all and everything. In my Christian days I would have called it "God". If I were a Buddhist I'd probably call it the Buddha-self. If I was a Taoist it would be The Tao. If I was a Hindu it might be Krishna or Brahman, if a Sufi, The Beloved or The Friend. As I am none of these, I call it 'Enabling Love.'

This is not a product of emotion or imagination though it is a palpable experience. Once your ego-self has been brought to rest your body will resonate with the peace, love and joy that emanates from the source of life within you. This will not be an emotional ecstasy or trance-like state. It will be a quiet contentment, gentle as gossamer, tender as a baby's touch. There is no force in it, no coercion present. Whereas your ego-awareness drives you, the True Self allures you; it is never obsessive and the experience never becomes an obsession. The Silence holds you tenderly just as gravity gently holds you to Mother Earth: not so tightly that you cannot move freely, not so loosely that you drift away.

At first this will be a brief experience. Your ego-awareness will impose itself again and this may be disappointing, but don't feel guilty or angry with yourself. Take time regularly during each day to pause and notice the presence within you. Once you have tasted it, you will not find it difficult to visit it again and again. The more you do this, the longer you will want to stay, but don't try to rush things. Allow this change to take place in you organically.

Over time your life will change though, at first, you may not notice it. We normalise our experiences very quickly. Think about going on holiday and how different and novel everything was when you first arrived, and how quickly it became normal as you found your way around. So it is with your experience of life, as your new sense of inner presence develops. You probably won't notice that you are any different until someone says, 'You're so relaxed these days.' Then you find that when someone says something provocative you are not provoked, and you think, 'Wow, I didn't blow my top like I used to.' The Tao Te Ching says that the presence of the Tao 'Untangles all knots and blunts all sharp edges.' In other words it alleviates my conflicts, so I am not a danger to myself and blunts my sharp edges, so I am not a danger to others.' It also says that for those who have learned to follow The Way, which I interpret as The True Self, 'a tiger will find no place to put its claws and a bull will find no place to put its horns.' When you are at peace with yourself you will be at peace with others too.

The Practices

The following practices will not induce an experience of inner peace. It's not possible to obtain genuine peace that way. But they will help to reduce the power of your ego-self and alleviate your habitual ego-awareness. This will free you to allow the Silence to do its job in you, a job you cannot accomplish yourself but can only allow to happen.

The Heartmath Exercise

You may find it beneficial to perform this little exercise, either before you begin any of the activities below or use it as a brief grounding practice as opportunity affords during the day. Researchers at the Heartmath Institute in California discovered that this action measurably synchronizes the heart-brain and the cerebral brain. It brings the sympathetic and para-sympathetic systems into harmony with each other.

> Concentrate on your heart for perhaps 10 or 15 seconds. Then bring to mind a dearly loved person. Speak to this person, either silently in your mind or out loud. Address this person by name and say, 'I love you. I long for you to be free from fear, anger, hatred and uncontrolled desire. I long for you to be filled with peace and love and joy.' Hold the image of that person and the intention of those words in your heart for a few moments.

Practice 1: Everyday Mindfulness

This is a good way to ease your way into stillness and you can practise this exercise doing any routine task in your working day. I like to do it when I'm washing up or unloading the dishwasher. You can use it when photocopying or filing or doing any routine manual job. It can be a prelude to other forms of meditation or used on its own. It's a good way to bring your mind back to the present moment after a testing meeting or a confrontation with someone. This is my dishwasher meditation:

Focus your attention on everything you do. Don't allow your mind to wander. If it does, bring it back gently to the matter in hand. Make every movement slowly and exercise great tenderness. Be conscious of how your body feels, as it moves slowly and deliberately. Bracket every action with a pause. Remember the Buddhist saying, 'Wherever you are, be there.'

Open the door of the dishwasher slowly and tenderly. Experience the joy of movement.

Remove a plate from the rack. Be conscious of the texture of the plate and the weight of it in your hand. Place it gently, even reverently, on the worktop. Remember to pause between each movement and be conscious of how that moment of stillness feels. Place each plate tenderly on the other, then take the stack carefully to the cupboard.

Open the cupboard slowly and tenderly. Be conscious of how the cupboard door feels, the way your body feels, how the plate feels. Pause for a moment and be conscious of the pause, then place the plate or the stack of plates in the cupboard tenderly.

Keep doing this until all the crockery, cutlery and utensils have been put away. By the time you've put everything away, you should feel thoroughly relaxed and calm, and it may then be appropriate to enter a period of silent meditation (see below).

Practice 2: 'Free Tai Chi'

I've built into this practice ideas from the Heartmath Institute. Recent research into the human heart has revealed it produces an energy field. This extends out from the body in all directions for about a metre. This means we are moving around inside a sort of bubble of energy, an aura, which flows around us. Most of us can't see this energy field but sensitive instruments can measure it. We are also intimately connected with everything else in the universe. Although the brain defines edges and makes everything appear separate to us, that isn't the quantum reality. As neurophysiologist, Jill Bolte Taylor says, we are energy fields which exist in an energy field and there's a way we can begin to experience this, at least imaginatively, though what we will be imagining is the actual reality.

Stand in an area where you have room to swing your arms around. Place your feet about shoulder-width apart, so you are standing firmly on the floor and bend your knees slightly. This is a traditional Tai Chi stance which provides stability. Close your eyes and take three breaths deep into your abdomen. Hold each breath briefly before expelling it as fully as possible. This will settle your body in a relaxed state.

Practice 2:1 Put your arms at about 45 degrees from your body. After a prolonged pause, move your arms in an arc upward and reach upwards toward the heavens. Look up and say, 'I am open'. Then bring your arms slowly down so they are stretching out on either side; bring them around before you in a gathering movement and say, 'to receive'. Then bring your hands back into the Namaste position, palms together pointing upwards with head bowed and fingertips touching your chin and say, 'With thanks.' Finally take your arms back to the 45 degree angle, palms facing forward and say, 'To share with the world.' Each of the four movements should be fluid and relaxed. You can repeat this as many times as you like.

Practice 2:2 This exercise will help synchronise your gross (physical) and subtle (emotional) bodies. Imagine yourself to be inside that bubble of heart energy in which you truly are. Slowly and gently, describe arcs with your arms. It's as if you are reaching out and touching the limits of your heart aura. Do this several times, sideways and forward. Realise your aura is even going into the ground below your feet, so you are, in fact, intimately connected with whatever is beneath your feet at all times.

Now, with your eyes closed and your feet planted firmly on the floor, begin to move your arms with gentle, flowing movements in any way you please. Imagine that at the ends of your fingers particles are being moved in the atmosphere around you—as they are. In your mind's eye see them making circles, like swirls in a pool of water—which, in fact, they are. Sometimes you may move each arm separately, sometimes in parallel, sometime as a mirror of each other. Don't think about it. Just let your body do what it wants to. Make every movement relatively slowly and make them smoothly, and tenderly. Concentrate on the movements and how your body feels. If thoughts drift into your mind, let them drift out again. Focus on what you are doing. This is fun. It's like consciously playing with gravity, quantum or maybe air molecules. It's also a practical way of experiencing yourself as part of the whole of existence, not an isolated individual. Keep this up for as long as you wish. Your body will probably tell you when it's had enough.

Practice 2:3 When I've been through a stressful experience, I find this exercise really useful. I imagine that whatever it was that made me stressed is a massive stone and, with both hands, I push it down and away from me. I have been amazed at how the seeming difficulty of this act is a measure of my level of peace. If pushing the stone away is easy, I know I've reached a place of peace. If it seems hard going, I know I need to meditate some more until I'm free of it.

Practice 2:4 I have no idea whether this will work for you. One day, standing with my eyes closed, I described a circle before me with my hands. I found I was imagining a great, translucent, milky-blue sphere. Although I was aware it was earth-sized, I seemed to be bigger than it. At first I felt I was on the edge of space with the earth before me and I reached out and began to tenderly touch the edge of the sphere. Gradually I realised that, although the image was earth-like, it had no continents and the milkiness blended with the translucent blueness. It was unlike the images I'd seen of clouds against the blue seas, when earth is seen from space. Then it occurred to me perhaps what I was looking at was not the earth but a representation of my own soul—the Self. I find this image appears each time I practise the exercise. It feels good to get up close and intimate with that otherwise intangible aspect of me*. I have noticed that when I'm in good spiritual fetter and carry out this exercise, my 'soul globe' (for want of a better word) seems huge. When I'm not so good, my 'soul globe' shrinks! (For me, this is a consistent experience. Don't ask me to explain.)

Practice 3: Meditation

You may find it helpful to have an automatic meditation bell. You can buy these, though I have to say some people have had difficulty with the timers. I use an mp3 version which I downloaded free from the internet and use with my mp3 player or laptop.

Meditation doesn't have to be silent. Many people repeat a mantra, a word or phrase spoken aloud over and over again. This helps the mind to concentrate intensely on the subject of the mantra (see below). Passage meditation is an extension of this technique, using a passage of scripture, a poem or a prayer. I learned about it from the late Eknath Easwaran's book, "Original Goodness" and adapted some of his ideas.

Find a quiet place where you will not be disturbed. Sit comfortably, either on a cushion on the floor or on an upright chair. Keep your back straight and your chin level. Close your eyes and

* I have met two other persons who have had similar experiences.

take three breaths deep into your abdomen. Hold each breath briefly before expelling it as fully as possible. Alternatively, you might use what Taoists call the 'microcosmic cycle'. When you breathe in, focus your awareness on the movement of the air, as it moves down your chest deep into the base of your torso. Pause very briefly and notice the feeling of stillness at that point, then breathe out, tracking the energies of the outward breath up your spine to the top of your head, pausing briefly when you come to your forehead. After three or as many of these breaths you want to take, breathe normally and be conscious of each breath.

Eknath suggests using the prayer of St. Francis but I don't do supplicatory prayer. So I've produced a version even someone like me can cope with. Here's my passage meditation.

May I be an instrument of light.
Where there is hatred, may I sow love;
Where there is injury, pardon;
Where there is doubt, faith;
Where there is despair, hope;
Where there is darkness, light;
Where there is sorrow, joy.
May I not so much seek to be consoled, but to console;
To be understood, but to understand;
To be loved, but to love.
For it is in giving that I receive;
It is in pardoning that I am pardoned;
It is in dying to self that I am born into eternal life.

If you're going to use the passage it is essential to memorise these words. Then, during the meditation, say the prayer very slowly and out loud, pausing after keywords, such as 'hatred', 'love', 'injury' and 'pardon'. Let the words drip their truth gently into your heart, as you focus all your consciousness on them. Pause for a minute or so between each recitation. Twenty or thirty minutes can fly by while you are engaged in this exercise.

I've also learned Paul's love poem from 1 Corinthians 13 and find this a helpful passage meditation.

Practice 4: Compassion Meditation

This is a meditation has been adapted from Joanna Macy's book *World as Lover, World as Self.* I've incorporated the Institute of Heartmath heart exercise.

> Find a quiet place where you will not be disturbed. Sit comfortably, either on a cushion on the floor or on an upright chair. Keep your back straight and your chin level. Close your eyes and take three breaths deep into your abdomen. Hold each breath briefly before expelling it as fully as possible. (Alternatively use the microcosmic cycle above).
>
> At this point, perform the Heartmath Exercise.
>
> Now bring to mind those who are closest to you in your family. Imagine them sitting before you in a semi-circle. Address each one by name and repeat the words above, or something similar. You can then bring in a wider range of friends and acquaintances into the circle, naming each one, then saying the words above to the whole gathering.
>
> There are likely to be some among your 'gathering' who have specific needs, in which case you can address those needs to that person. As an alternative I've sometimes spoken the prayer of St. Francis to each individual or group, changing the 'I' to 'you'.
>
> Another alternative I use regularly is to focus my attention on an individual with the greatest need and speak my longing for that

need to be met directly to that person. Someone remarked that this is cutting "God" out. I replied that it is "God" that is enabling compassion in me and this action is more like "God" speaking to "God" about "God".

Practice 5: Thankfulness Meditation
This is adapted from an idea by Thich Nhat Hanh. It can be used in relation to any object.

Place any object before you, and perform the Heartmath Exercise. Now focus on the object and imagine the different people, machines, plants and materials which went into producing it. Just say thank you to each person, machine, plant or piece of material for their part in bringing the object to you. For instance, with a book before you, you might say:

Thank you, sun, for making clouds.
Thank you, sea, for surrendering your waters.
Thank you, clouds, for bringing rain.
Thank you, rain, for watering the earth.
Thank you, earth, for producing the trees which made us these books.
Thank you, lumberjack, for felling the tree.
Thank you, lorry-driver, for conveying the tree to the mill.
Thank you, engineers, for designing the mill and builders for building it.
Thank you, chemists, for your part in the production.
. . . and so on.

You don't have to say the words 'thank you'; just hold an attitude of gratitude in your heart, as you think of each person or element. The list is almost endless and you begin to realise how many people and elements have been involved, just so that you can have that book on your shelf. It is likely to deepen your sense of oneness and gratitude. Remember, not to do this exercise with any expectation of an outcome.

Practice 5:2 It's good to do this exercise during a meal. Porridge becomes quite profound. Open your full consciousness to what you are eating, to what it looks like, smells like, tastes like and feels like. Savour the taste and texture of the food in your mouth. Eat slowly. Think about the people who were involved in bringing the food to your plate. Consider the abundance of Mother Earth, the nurturing of the weather and the care of the grower. Imagine the skill of those who packaged it and transported it, and the service of those who stocked it and sold it to you. Be grateful to each one for their part in feeding you. Above all, realise that for you to remain alive, something has to die every day.

Practice 6: The Mantra

The mantra has been used in most religions for thousands of years. You can use it to help you enter a meditative state or, in times of crisis, to bring you into consciousness of the present moment. It's useful in times of temptation or to keep your mind from wandering while you are walking or going about your business during the day.

The content of the mantra is not vitally important, though something devotional is usually best. Christians, Jews, Muslims and Hindus have used the name, or one of the names of "God". I have found 'Enabling Love', my own name for "God", to be useful. One version is a rhythmic recitation of 'Enabling Love, Enabling Love, enable me.' Another useful mantra is in Sanskrit: *Tat Tvam Asi* ('That Thou Art'). There's also a passage from the Upanishads: 'I am the Lord of Love.'

The mantra is rumbling away within me as I walk along. I see a flower and the mantra reminds me it is enabled by love. I see a lorry and that is enabled by love too, as is that building, those traffic lights, that tree, those people—and so on. I found it to be a good thing to do in hospital, when I was undergoing scans, preparing to go into theatre and when I was surrounded by machinery in the intensive care ward afterwards. It was good to remind myself that the surgeons who operated and all the equipment they used, were enabled by that love which is at the heart of the universe and at the heart of me.

The quotation from the Upanishads, 'I am the Lord of Love,' I have put into a rhythmic phrase: 'I am the Lord, the Lord, the Lord, I am the Lord of Love.' I've even set it to music and find this a useful accompaniment to a brisk walk.

For meditation, sounding the traditional word OM (pronounced AUM) is a useful experience. Take a deep breath then, as you are breathing out, make the sound beginning at the back of the throat with the mouth open. As you close your mouth slowly, listen to the sound change in character—from a flat 'Ah' to an 'Au' to the finishing 'Mm'.. The lower the tone, the better. Some Buddhist monks can get a really deep and resonant sound. OM is composed of three sounds: A U and M. In the Mandukya Upanishad 'A' represents the world of waking consciousness, 'U' the world of dreaming sleep and 'M' dreamless sleep in which the knower is united with the known—the lover with the beloved. This is the object of meditation, to move us from waking consciousness to consciousness of what we may refer to as "God".

Loving Kindness Meditation

I've added this practice to the second edition because I've found it to be one of the most powerful of the practices I use.

> First relax your body and calm your mind, perhaps using the Heartmath exercise.
>
> Open yourself, be receptive and speak these words slowly and mindfully:

"May I be whole. May I be well.
May I be filled with peace, love and joy."

Do this three times.

Then focus on someone in in need and speak slowly and mindfully:

"May you be whole. May you be well.
May you be filled with peace, love and joy."

You can spend time focusing your attention on individuals and groups of people speaking these words to them out of your heart. The circle of people you involve can widen and widen reaching local, national and world leaders and influencers.

***

Such spiritual practices described above are not meant to bring you into an ecstatic experience of the divine, though, by grace, this may happen from time to time. For me, they help, day by day, to avoid having a mind full of anxieties, fears, resentments, bitterness or anything which hinders my well-being and spiritual progress. They help to bring clarity and peace through detachment. When I'm confronted with a difficult situation, I'm usually able to respond appropriately. (But I still have my moments!).

As a result of such exercises you should find yourself not so prone to react out of the instincts of the primitive lower brain. When someone becomes angry, you may well find that you don't automatically get angry or defensive in response. If someone takes a particular political stance on something you don't agree with, you may realise that it's not that important and choose not to argue. Things that concerned or annoyed you, were tempted you or repelled you, may be lesser in their effect or have no affect at all. It's not that you are indifferent to such things, just that the ego-self no longer needs the hyper-stimulation, approbation or self-satisfaction to make it feel safe and happy. We find a spring of inner joy that is always present and accessible. You no longer need to *pursue happiness* because you have found your own source of peace, love and joy.

If you continue on this trajectory you may reach a place where spiritual practices are no longer necessary. You will have been enabled to enter a state of grace in which the mind is no longer subject to the distractions by the ego-self. But don't aim for that state. Desire it but don't be ambitious for anything. That only leads to dissatisfaction. Just be prepared for what arises and observe it. When you can do this fairly consistently you will know that you know, although you will never know what you know.

Namaste.

Printed in Great Britain
by Amazon

86844218R00129